Practice Papers for SQA Exams

National 5

Biology

© 2014 Leckie & Leckie Ltd
001/15012014

10 9 8 7 6 5 4 3 2

ISBN 9780007504725

Published by
Leckie & Leckie Ltd
An imprint of HarperCollins*Publishers*
Westerhill Road, Bishopbriggs, Glasgow, G64 2QT
T: 0844 576 8126   F: 0844 576 8131
leckieandleckie@harpercollins.co.uk

www.leckieandleckie.co.uk

Special thanks to
QBS (layout and illustration); Ink Tank (cover design); Jill Laidlaw (copy-edit); Paul Sensecall (proofread); Rona Gloag (proofread)

A CIP Catalogue record for this book is available from the British Library.

Acknowledgements
Whilst every effort has been made to trace the copyright holders, in cases where this has been unsuccessful, or if any have inadvertently been overlooked, the Publishers would gladly receive any information enabling them to rectify any error or omission at the first opportunity.

Cover image © Lculig

Printed in Italy by Grafica Veneta S.p.A.

Introduction

The three papers included in this book are designed to provide practice in the National 5 Biology course assessment question paper (the examination), which is worth 80% of the final grade for this course.

Together, the three papers give overall and comprehensive coverage of the assessment of **knowledge and its application** as well as the **skills of scientific inquiry** needed to pass National 5 Biology. The **Key Area Index** grid on page 5 shows the pattern of coverage of the knowledge in the key areas and the skills across the three papers.

We recommend that candidates download a copy of the course assessment specification from the SQA website at www.sqa.org.uk. Print pages 8–12, which summarise the knowledge and skills that will be tested.

Design of the papers

Each paper has been carefully assembled to be very similar to a typical National 5 question paper. Each paper has 80 marks and is divided into two sections.

- **Section 1** – objective test, which contains 20 multiple choice items worth 1 mark each, totalling 20 marks.

- **Section 2** – paper 2, which contains restricted and extended response questions worth 1 to 3 marks each, totalling 60 marks.

In each paper, the marks are distributed evenly across all three component units of the course, and the majority of the marks are for the demonstration and application of knowledge. The other marks are for the application of skills of scientific inquiry. We have included features of the national papers such as offering choice in some questions and building in opportunities for candidates to suggest adjustments to investigation and experimental designs.

Most questions in each paper are set at the standard of Grade C, but there are also more difficult questions set at the standard for Grade A. We have attempted to construct each paper to represent the typical range of demand in a National 5 Biology paper.

Using the papers

Each paper can be attempted as a whole, or groups of questions on a particular topic or skill area can be tackled – use the **Key Area Index** grid to find related groups of questions. In the grid, questions may appear twice if they cover more than one skill area. Use the 'Date completed' column to keep a record of your progress.

We recommend working between attempting the questions and studying their expected answers.

You will need a **pen**, a **sharp pencil**, **a clear plastic ruler** and a **calculator** for the best results. A couple of different **coloured highlighters** could also be handy.

Expected answers

The expected answers on pages 83–103 give national standard answers but, occasionally, there may be other acceptable answers. The answers have Top Tips provided alongside each one but don't feel you need to use them all!

The Top Tips include hints on the biology itself as well as some memory ideas, a focus on traditionally difficult areas, advice on the wording of answers and notes of commonly made errors.

Grading

The three papers are designed to be equally demanding and to reflect the national standard of a typical SQA paper. Each paper has 80 marks – if you score 40 marks, that's a C pass. You will need about 48 marks for a B pass and about 56 marks for an A. These figures are a rough guide only.

Timing

If you are attempting a full paper, limit yourself to **two hours** to complete. Get someone to time you! We recommend no more than 25 minutes for **Section 1** and the remainder of the time for **Section 2**.

If you are tackling blocks of questions, give yourself about a minute and a half per mark, for example, 10 marks of questions should take no longer than 15 minutes.

Good luck!

Topic index

Skill tested	Key area	Practice paper questions S1 – Section 1 S2 – Section 2			Date completed
		Exam A	*Exam B*	*Exam C*	
Unit 1: Cell biology Demonstrating and applying knowledge	1. Cell structure	**S1:** 1 **S2:** –	**S1:** 1 **S2:** –	**S1:** – **S2:** 1a, b, c, d	
	2. Transport across cell membranes	**S1:** 4 **S2:** 1a, b, c, d	**S1:** – **S2:** 1a, b, c	**S1:** 1, 2 **S2:** 2a, 2 bii	
	3. Producing new cells	**S1:** 5 **S2:** –	**S1:** – **S2:** 2a, b, c	**S1:** 5 **S2:** –	
	4. DNA and the production of proteins	**S1:** 6 **S2:** –	**S1:** – **S2:** 3a, b, c, d, e	**S1:** 3 **S2:** –	
	5. Proteins and enzymes	**S1:** – **S2:** 2a, b, c	**S1:** 3 **S2:** –	**S1:** 4 **S2:** –	
	6. Genetic engineering	**S1:** 7 **S2:** –	**S1:** 4 **S2:** –	**S1:** – **S2:** 3a, b, c, d	
	7. Photosynthesis	**S1:** – **S2:** 3a	**S1:** 5, 6 **S2:** – 12c	**S1:** 6 **S2:** –	
	8. Respiration	**S1:** – **S2:** 4b	**S1:** 7 **S2:** 4c	**S1:** 14 **S2:** –	
Unit 2: Multicellular organisms Demonstrating and applying knowledge	1. Cells, tissues and organs	**S1:** 8 **S2:** –	**S1:** – **S2:** 1d	**S1:** – **S2:** 4d	
	2. Stem cells and meristems	**S1:** 9 **S2:** –	**S1:** 9 **S2:** –	**S1:** 12 **S2:** –	
	3. Control and communication	**S1:** 10, 11 **S2:** 5a, b, c	**S1:** – **S2:** 5a, b, c, d	**S1:** 8 **S2:** 5a, b, c	
	4. Reproduction	**S1:** 12 **S2:** –	**S1:** 12 **S2:** –	**S1:** 9 **S2:** –	
	5. Variation and inheritance	**S1:** – **S2:** 6a, b	**S1:** 10, 11 **S2:** 6b, c	**S1:** 10 **S2:** 6c	
	6. The need for transport	**S1:** 13 **S2:** 7a, b, 8a, b	**S1:** 13, 14 **S2:** 7a, b, c, d, 8 b, c, d	**S1:** 11, 13 **S2:** 7a	
	7. Lifestyle choices	**S1:** – **S2:** –	**S1:** – **S2:** –	**S1:** – **S2:** –	

Unit 3: Life on Earth Demonstrating and applying knowledge	1. Biodiversity and distribution of life	**S1:** 14, 15, 16, **S2:** –	**S1:** 15 **S2:** –	**S1:** 15 **S2:** 9a, c	
	2. Energy in ecosystems	**S1:** 18 **S2:** 11a, b, c	**S1:** 16 **S2:** 10a, b, c	**S1:** 16, 17 **S2:** 12a, b, c	
	3. Sampling and measurement	**S1:** – **S2:** 10d	**S1:** – **S2:** 9a	**S1:** – **S2:** 10a, c	
	4. Adaptation and evolution	**S1:** – **S2:** 9b, c	**S1:** 18 **S2:** 11a, b	**S1:** – **S2:** 11a, b	
	5. Human impact on the environment	**S1:** – **S2:** 12a, b	**S1:** – **S2:** 10c	**S1:** 19 **S2:** 12d	
N5 Biology Course Skills of scientific inquiry	• Planning investigations	**S1:** 20 **S2:** 3bii, biii, 10a	**S1:** 8 **S2:** 4e	**S1:** – **S2:** 4c, 6a, 8a, b	
	• Selecting information	**S1:** 2 **S2:** 8ci, 9a	**S1:** 19 **S2:** 8a, 9b, c, d, 12b	**S1:** 18 **S2:** 6b, 7bi, bii	
	• Presenting information	**S1:** – **S2:** 4a	**S1:** – **S2:** 4a	**S1:** – **S2:** 2bi	
	• Processing information	**S1:** 2, 13, 17, 19 **S2:** 8cii, 10b	**S1:** 2, 19 **S2:** 4b, 6a	**S1:** 20 **S2:** 2biii, 4a, 7bi, bii, 9b	
	• Predicting and generalising	**S1:** – **S2:** 3bi, 4d, 10c	**S1:** – **S2:** 1a	**S1:** 1 **S2:** –	
	• Concluding and explaining	**S1:** 3 **S2:** 3bi, 12c, d	**S1:** 17, 20 **S2:** 6b, 9a, 12a	**S1:** 7 **S2:** 4b, 6c	
	• Evaluating	**S1:** – **S2:** 4c	**S1:** – **S2:** 4d	**S1:** – **S2:** 10b	

Practice Exam A

SECTION 1 ANSWER GRID

Mark the correct answer as shown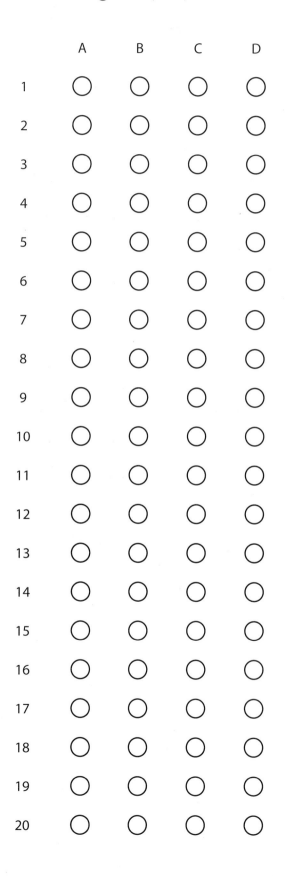

	A	B	C	D
1	○	○	○	○
2	○	○	○	○
3	○	○	○	○
4	○	○	○	○
5	○	○	○	○
6	○	○	○	○
7	○	○	○	○
8	○	○	○	○
9	○	○	○	○
10	○	○	○	○
11	○	○	○	○
12	○	○	○	○
13	○	○	○	○
14	○	○	○	○
15	○	○	○	○
16	○	○	○	○
17	○	○	○	○
18	○	○	○	○
19	○	○	○	○
20	○	○	○	○

N5 Biology

Practice Papers for SQA Exams   Section 1 – Questions

Fill in these boxes and read what is printed below.

Full name of centre   Town

Forename(s)   Surname

Try to answer ALL of the questions in the time allowed.

You have 2 hours to complete this paper.

Write your answers in the spaces provided, including all of your working.

SECTION 1

1. The diagram below shows some structures present in a mesophyll cell from a green plant.

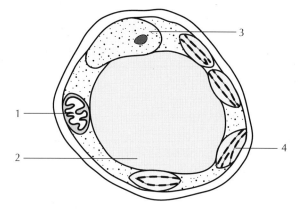

Which line in the table below identifies correctly the structures in the cell that carry out photosynthesis and contain genetic information?

	Carry out photosynthesis	*Contain genetic information*
A	1	2
B	4	3
C	1	3
D	4	2

2. The histogram below shows the number of cells of different lengths in a sample of onion epidermis.

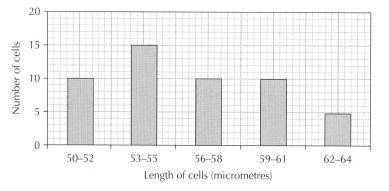

What percentage of the cells in the sample have a length greater than 58 micrometres?

A 15%

B 25%

C 30%

D 50%.

3. 50 mm strips of potato tissue were placed into each of three sucrose solutions P, Q and R of different concentrations and left at room temperature. After 1 hour the strips of tissue were re-measured and the results are shown in the table below.

Sucrose solution	Length of potato tissue strip after 1 hour (mm)
P	50
Q	47
R	52

Which of the following conclusions based on these results is valid?

A Solution P had a lower concentration of sucrose than the potato cell sap

B Solution Q had a higher concentration of sucrose than the potato cell sap

C Solution R had a higher concentration of sucrose than the potato cell sap

D Solutions P, Q and R had the same concentration as the potato cell sap.

4. In active transport, molecules are moved by membrane

A proteins against the concentration gradient

B lipids down the concentration gradient

C lipids against the concentration gradient

D proteins down the concentration gradient.

5. The diagram below shows a stage in mitosis in a plant cell.

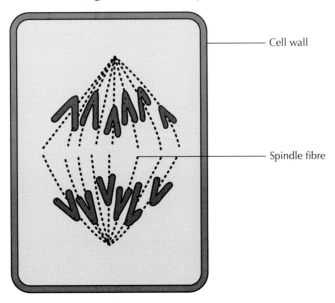

Cell wall

Spindle fibre

Which of the following best describes the chromosomes at the stage of mitosis shown? The chromosomes have

A become visible as pairs of identical chromatids

B aligned at the equator of the spindle

C gathered at opposite poles of the spindle

D been pulled apart by spindle fibres.

6. The diagram below represents a short piece of a DNA molecule.

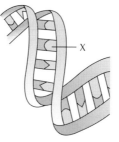

Which part of the DNA molecule is shown at X?

A Sugar

B Base

C Gene

D Amino acid.

7. The diagram below shows a genetically modified bacterial cell that contains a human gene.

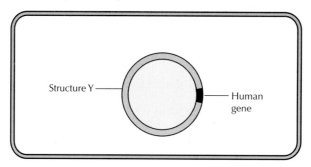

Structure Y, which contains the human gene, is

A the nucleus

B a chromosome

C a ribosome

D a plasmid.

8. A group of similar cells working together to perform the same function is called

A an organism

B a system

C an organ

D a tissue.

9. Which of the following statements is **false** in relation to stem cells?

Stem cells

A are found in animal embryos

B can undergo cell division

C develop into gametes

D can produce new stem cells.

10. The diagram below shows a vertical section through the human brain.

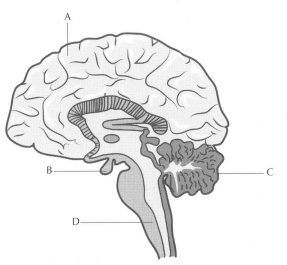

Which letter indicates the site of memory storage and reasoning?

11. Which organ contains target tissues that respond to insulin?

A Small intestine

B Pancreas

C Liver

D Brain.

12. Which line in the table below shows correctly the chromosome complements of the mammalian cells listed?

	Mammalian cell		
	muscle cell	gamete	zygote
A	diploid	haploid	haploid
B	diploid	haploid	diploid
C	haploid	diploid	diploid
D	haploid	diploid	haploid

13. The cardiac output from the heart is calculated using the equation shown below.

cardiac output (litres per min) = volume of blood pumped per beat (cm³) × heart rate (beats per minute)

A hospital patient had a heart rate of 80 beats per minute and a cardiac output of 4 litres per minute.

What is the volume of blood pumped per beat?

A 5 cm³

B 20 cm³

C 50 cm³

D 320 cm³.

14. The total variety of all living organisms on Earth is described as its

A biome

B biodiversity

C ecosystem

D population.

15. Which of the following statements is **true**?

A Scottish moorland community consists of all of the

A plant species present

B plants species present and the non-living environment

C plant and animal species present and the non-living environment

D plant and animal species present.

16. Which of the following factors are **both** biotic?

A Predation and temperature

B Temperature and pH

C pH and grazing

D Grazing and predation.

17. Between each level in a food chain 90% of energy is lost.

In the food chain below, the plant plankton contains 100 000 units of energy gained by photosynthesis.

plant plankton $\rightarrow$ **animal plankton** $\rightarrow$ **small fish** $\rightarrow$ **predatory fish**

How many energy units would be found in the predatory fish?

A 10 000

B 1 000

C 100

D 10.

18. Bacteria present in the root nodules of clover plants are beneficial to the plants because they

A convert atmospheric nitrogen to nitrates

B convert ammonia to nitrite

C remove nitrogen from roots and release it to soil

D synthesise protein for plant cells.

Questions 19 and 20 refer to the following information.

A survey of the number of limpets on rocky areas of a seashore was carried out using quadrats.

The squares in the diagram below indicate the number of limpets recorded in each quadrat.

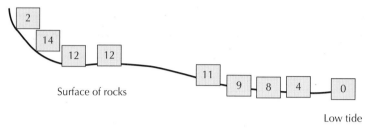

19. What is the average number of limpets per quadrat?

    A 8

    B 9

    C 11

    D 12.

20. Which of the following is a precaution needed to make the results of the survey more valid?

    A Place quadrats randomly

    B Use exactly ten quadrats

    C Place quadrats where limpets occurred

    D Repeat the quadrat sampling several times.

N5 Biology

Practice Papers for SQA Exams

Section 2 – Questions

Fill in these boxes and read what is printed below.

Full name of centre

Town

Forename(s)

Surname

Try to answer ALL of the questions in the time allowed.

You have 2 hours to complete this paper.

Write your answers in the spaces provided, including all of your working.

Scotland's leading educational publishers

SECTION 2

1. The diagram below represents molecules present in a magnified fragment of cell membrane.

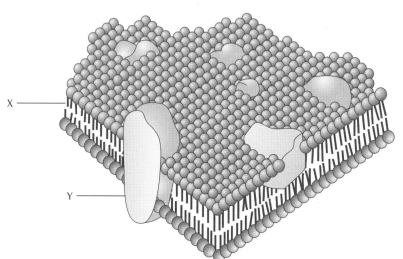

(a) Name molecules X and Y.

X _____

Y _____

2

(b) Complete the following sentences by <u>underlining</u> the correct options in each choice bracket.

The cell membrane is $\left\{ \begin{array}{c} \text{selectively} \\ \text{fully} \end{array} \right\}$ permeable and transports water in and out of the cell by osmosis.

Osmotic movement occurs $\left\{ \begin{array}{c} \text{down} \\ \text{against} \end{array} \right\}$ the concentration gradient and

and $\left\{ \begin{array}{c} \text{requires} \\ \text{does not require} \end{array} \right\}$ energy.

2

(c) The diagram below shows a cell from a piece of plant tissue.

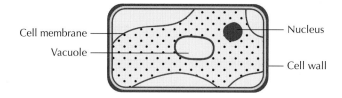

(i) Describe how a piece of plant tissue could be treated so that its cells appeared as shown in the diagram.

_____

_____

1

(ii) Give the term applied to cells that appear as shown in the diagram.

_____

1

Total marks 6

2. The diagrams below represent stages in a synthesis (building up) reaction catalysed by a human enzyme molecule at 37 °C.

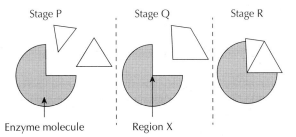

(a) Complete the flow chart below by adding letters to show the correct order of these stages as they would occur during the reaction.

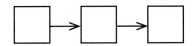

1

(b) Identify the part of the enzyme molecule labelled region X in the diagram.

_____

1

(c) Explain why the cellular reaction above would **not** occur if the temperature were increased to 60 °C

_____

_____

2

Total marks 4

3. (a) The diagram below shows parts of two stages of photosynthesis in a green plant.

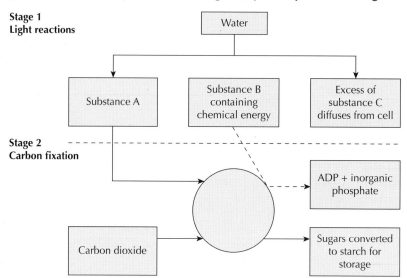

Complete the table below by naming substances A, B and C produced during Stage 1.

Substance	Name
A	
B	
C	

2

(b) The apparatus in the diagram below was used to investigate the requirements for photosynthesis in a green plant.

The plant was kept in darkness for 24 hours before being placed in bright light for 5 hours.

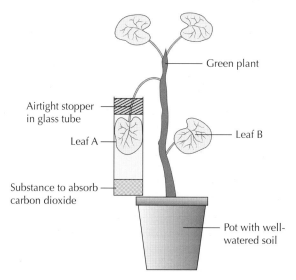

(i)   After the apparatus had been in bright light for 5 hours, a test for starch was carried out on **leaf A**.

Predict the result of this test and give a valid conclusion about the requirements for photosynthesis that can be drawn from it.

Result _____   **1**

Conclusion _____

_____   **1**

(ii) Describe how **leaf B** would be treated so that it could act as a control in this experiment.

_____

_____   **1**

(iii) Describe how the apparatus could be altered to show that light is needed for photosynthesis.

_____

_____   **1**

_____

Total marks 6

4.   An investigation was carried out on the effect of temperature on the rate of fermentation in yeast.

Apparatus as shown in the diagram below was set up, and the number of bubbles of gas produced by the yeast per minute was counted at various temperatures, as shown in the table.

Apparatus

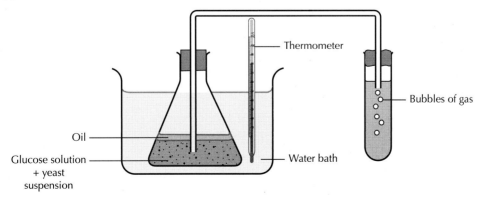

Temperature (°C)	Bubbles of gas produced per minute
10	30
15	50
20	80
25	110
30	120

(a) On the grid provided below, draw a line graph of temperature against number of bubbles of gas produced per minute.

(A spare grid, if required, can be found on page 31.)

2

(b) Identify the gas produced during fermentation.

_____ **1**

(c) Suggest how the investigation could be improved to give more accurate results.

_____

_____ **1**

MARKS
Do not write in this margin

(d) Predict how the results would be different if the investigation were repeated at 5 °C. Explain your answer.

Prediction ____ 1

Explanation

____

____ 1

Total marks 6

5. The diagram below shows a reflex arc in a human and the neurons involved.

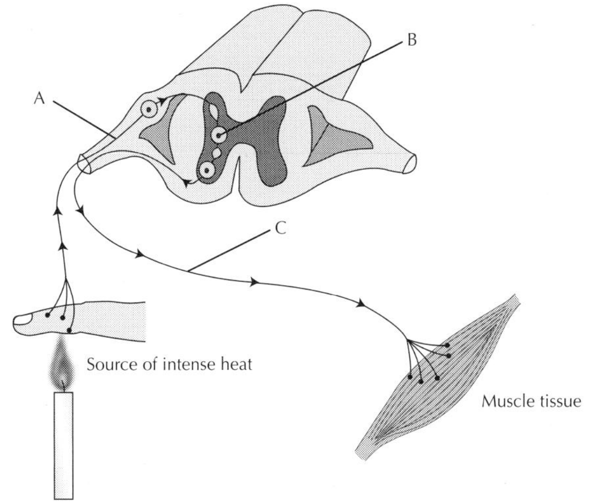
B
A
C
Source of intense heat
Muscle tissue

(a) Identify the type of neuron shown at A.

________________________ 1

(b) Name the gap at B and describe the role of chemicals that enter this gap.

Name ________________________

Role ____ 2

(c) Explain the advantage of this reflex to the human involved.

____

____ 2

Total marks 5

6. Tongue rolling in humans is controlled by a single gene.
The dominant allele is tongue-rolling (**R**) and the recessive allele is non-rolling (**r**).

The diagram below shows the inheritance of tongue-rolling in part of a family.

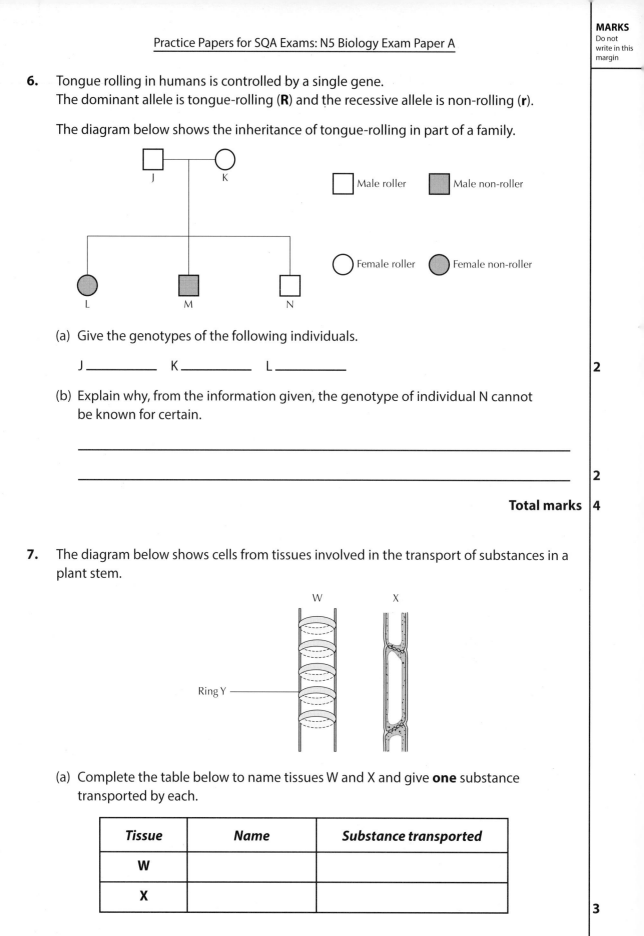

(a) Give the genotypes of the following individuals.

J _____ K _____ L _____   **2**

(b) Explain why, from the information given, the genotype of individual N cannot be known for certain.

_____

_____   **2**

Total marks 4

7. The diagram below shows cells from tissues involved in the transport of substances in a plant stem.

(a) Complete the table below to name tissues W and X and give **one** substance transported by each.

Tissue	Name	Substance transported
W		
X		

3

(b) Name the substance of which ring Y is composed.

_____ **1**

Total marks **4**

8. The diagram below shows part of the human breathing system.

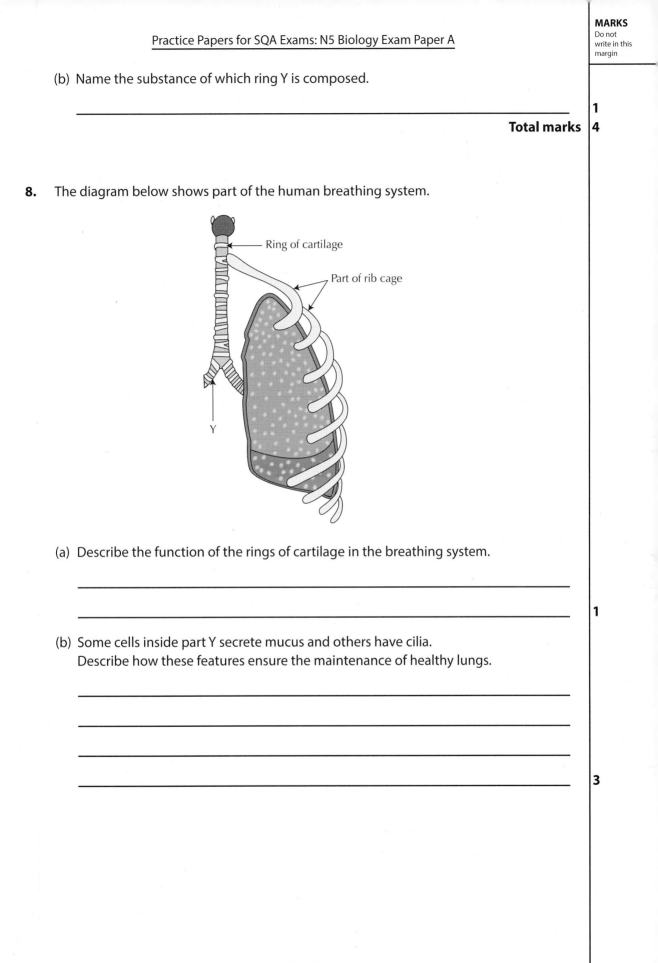

Ring of cartilage

Part of rib cage

Y

(a) Describe the function of the rings of cartilage in the breathing system.

_____

_____ **1**

(b) Some cells inside part Y secrete mucus and others have cilia.
Describe how these features ensure the maintenance of healthy lungs.

_____

_____

_____

_____ **3**

(c) The chart below shows some information relating to the annual death rate of males in an area of the UK from coronary heart disease over the course of one year.

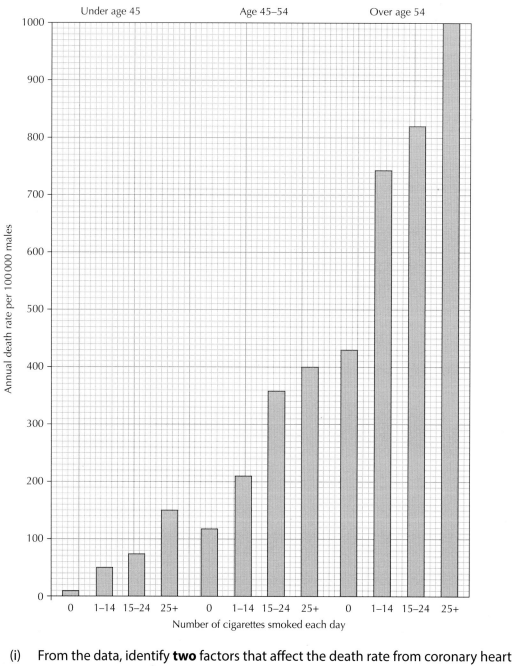

(i) From the data, identify **two** factors that affect the death rate from coronary heart disease.

1 _____

2 _____

1

(ii) Calculate the percentage increase in death rate in males under 45 years when the number of cigarettes smoked per day is increased from 1–14 to 25+.

Space for calculations

_____% **1**

Total marks 6

9. The table and diagrams below give information about the beaks of two species of finch and a description of the habitats they occupy on the Galapagos Islands.

Size and shape of beak	Description of habitat
wide, deep and blunt	woodland with flowering shrubs providing large seeds and nuts
long, narrow and pointed	woodland with rotting logs providing food for insects

Finch species P

Finch species Q

(a) Identify the finch species that eats large seeds and give a reason for your choice.

Species _____

Reason _____

_____ **1**

(b) Suggest **two** ways in which competition between the two species is reduced.

1 _____

2 _____ **2**

(c) These two species may have arisen by evolution from a common ancestor. The processes below are involved in the formation of new species.

P mutation

Q natural selection

R isolation

Complete the flow chart below by adding the letters to show the order in which these processes would have occurred to produce the two species of finch.

1

Total marks 4

10. The bar charts below show the results of an investigation carried out to compare the numbers of four different species of ground layer plants in a hectare of woodland with the numbers found in a hectare of grassland nearby.

(1 hectare = 10 000 m²)

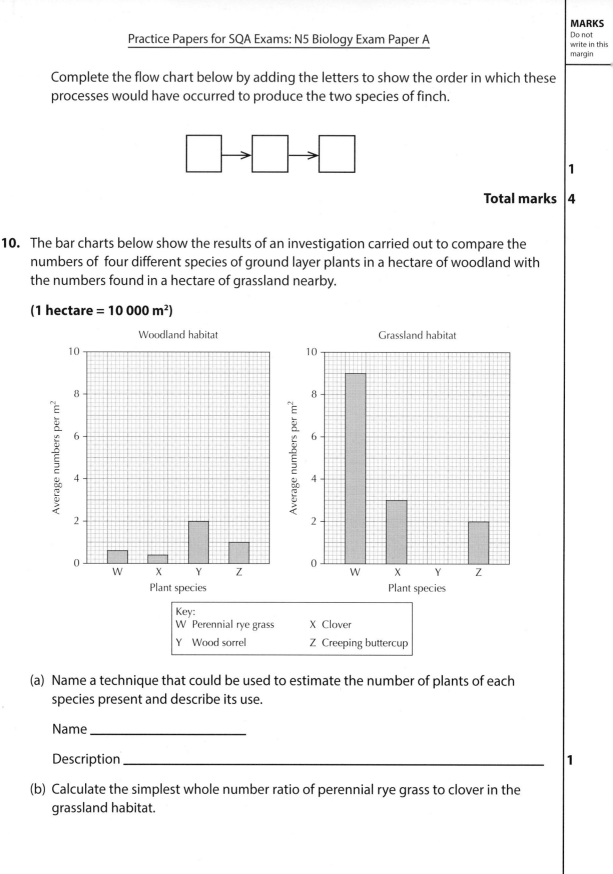

(a) Name a technique that could be used to estimate the number of plants of each species present and describe its use.

Name _____

Description _____ 1

(b) Calculate the simplest whole number ratio of perennial rye grass to clover in the grassland habitat.

_____ : _____
perennial rye grass   clover

1

(c) Estimate the total number of wood sorrel plants that would be present in the entire hectare of woodland.

Space for calculations

_____ plants   **1**

(d) **Choose** an abiotic factor that might be involved in the different abundance of perennial rye grass in these two habitats and explain its role.

Abiotic factor _____

Explanation _____

_____   **2**

Total marks   **5**

11. The diagram below shows part of the nitrogen cycle.

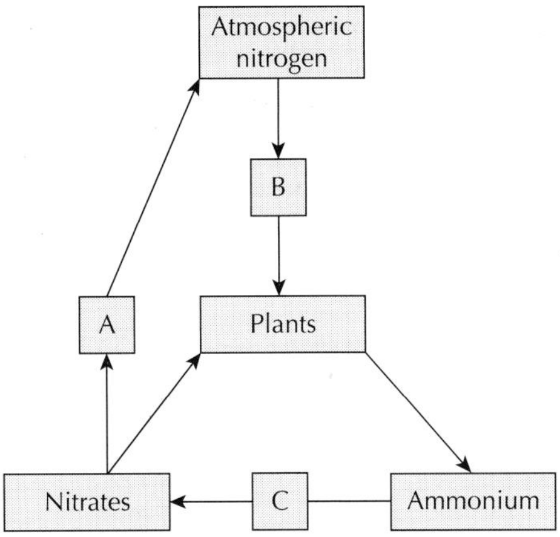

(a) Complete the table by inserting **one** letter from the diagram into each box to show the type of bacteria involved at each of the stages shown in the diagram.

Type of bacteria involved	Letter
nitrogen-fixing bacteria	
nitrifying bacteria	
denitrifying bacteria	

2

(b) Name **one** type of substance found in plants that is produced using nitrates taken up from the soil.

_____

1

(c) Give the general name for organisms that can produce ammonium from plant remains.

_____

1

Total marks **4**

12. The graph below shows the concentration of dissolved oxygen and nitrate together with the numbers of algal cells present at various sampling positions along a river near the outfall from a sewage pipe.

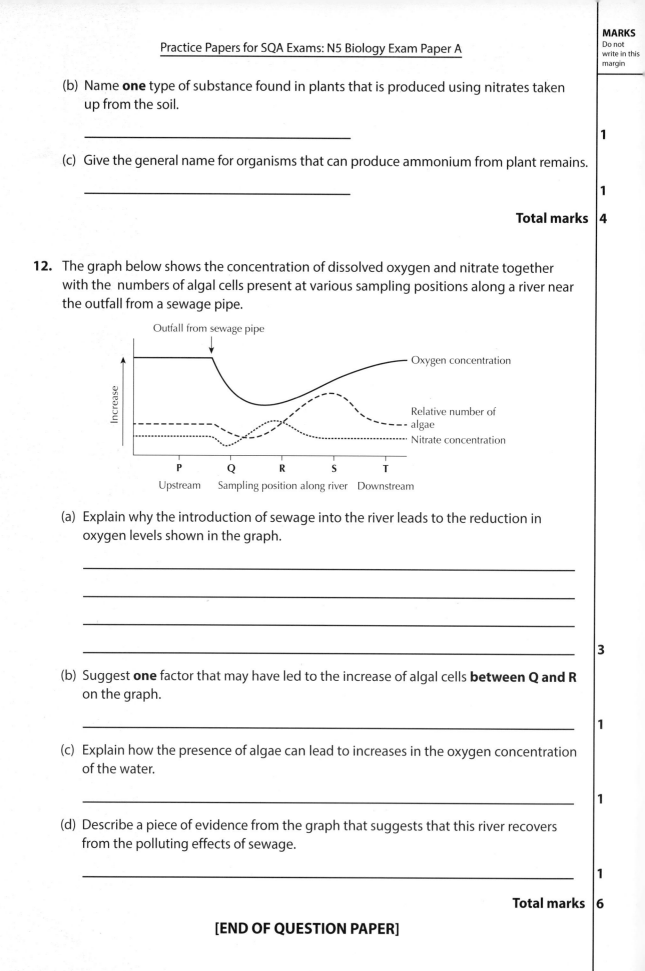

(a) Explain why the introduction of sewage into the river leads to the reduction in oxygen levels shown in the graph.

_____

_____

_____

_____

3

(b) Suggest **one** factor that may have led to the increase of algal cells **between Q and R** on the graph.

_____

1

(c) Explain how the presence of algae can lead to increases in the oxygen concentration of the water.

_____

1

(d) Describe a piece of evidence from the graph that suggests that this river recovers from the polluting effects of sewage.

_____

1

Total marks **6**

[END OF QUESTION PAPER]

ADDITIONAL GRAPH PAPER

SECTION 1 ANSWER GRID

Mark the correct answer as shown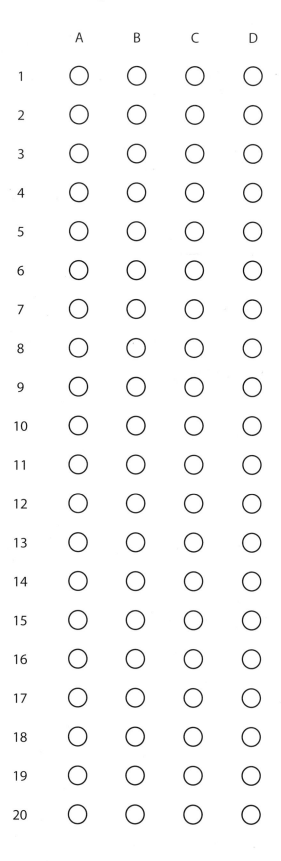

	A	B	C	D
1	○	○	○	○
2	○	○	○	○
3	○	○	○	○
4	○	○	○	○
5	○	○	○	○
6	○	○	○	○
7	○	○	○	○
8	○	○	○	○
9	○	○	○	○
10	○	○	○	○
11	○	○	○	○
12	○	○	○	○
13	○	○	○	○
14	○	○	○	○
15	○	○	○	○
16	○	○	○	○
17	○	○	○	○
18	○	○	○	○
19	○	○	○	○
20	○	○	○	○

N5 Biology

Practice Papers for SQA Exams

Section 1 – Questions

Fill in these boxes and read what is printed below.

Full name of centre

Town

Forename(s)

Surname

Try to answer ALL of the questions in the time allowed.

You have 2 hours to complete this paper.

Write your answers in the spaces provided, including all of your working.

Scotland's leading educational publishers

SECTION 1

1. The diagram below shows some structures present in a fungal cell.

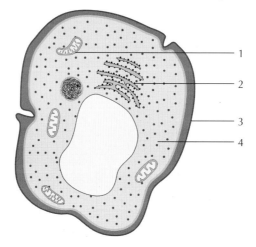

Which line in the table below identifies correctly the site of aerobic respiration and the structure that provides support for the cell?

	Site of aerobic respiration	*Provides support for cell*
A	1	4
B	2	3
C	2	4
D	1	3

2. The diagram below shows cells in a piece of onion epidermal tissue as seen under a microscope.

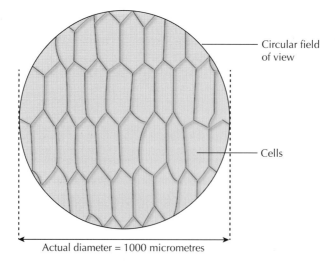

Circular field of view

Cells

Actual diameter = 1000 micrometres

The best estimate of the average **length** of the cells shown is

A   10 micrometres

B   25 micrometres

C   100 micrometres

D   250 micrometres.

3.   Which line in the table below shows correctly the terms that apply to the descriptions of enzyme action given?

	Description of enzyme action	
	best conditions for enzyme action	*effect of reaction on enzyme molecules*
A	optimum	denatured
B	specific	unchanged
C	optimum	unchanged
D	specific	denatured

4.   The following are stages in the genetic engineering of bacteria.

1   Insert plasmid into host cell

2   Extract required gene from chromosome

3   Insert required gene into plasmid

4   Remove plasmid from host cell.

Which is the correct sequence of stages that would be carried out during the process of genetic modification of the bacteria?

A   2→4→1→3

B   2→4→3→1

C   3→4→1→2

D   3→1→4→2.

5. The apparatus below was set up to investigate photosynthesis in an aquatic plant.

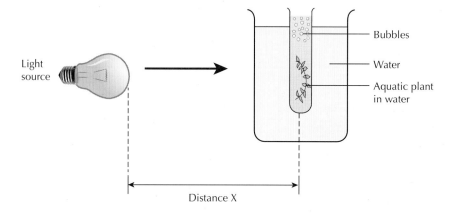

The list below shows variables related to photosynthesis that could be measured.

1 Light intensity

2 Rate of carbon fixation

3 Rate of bubble production

If distance X was increased, which variable(s) on the list would **decrease**?

A 1 only

B 2 only

C 1 and 3 only

D 1, 2 and 3.

6. The role of chlorophyll in photosynthesis is to trap

A light energy for ATP production

B light energy for carbon dioxide absorption

C chemical energy for carbon dioxide absorption

D chemical energy for ATP production.

7. The diagram below shows respiratory pathways in a mammalian muscle cell.

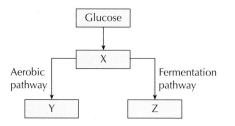

Which line in the table below identifies correctly substance(s) in boxes X, Y and Z?

	X	Y	Z
A	pyruvate	carbon dioxide and water	lactic acid
B	pyruvate	lactic acid	carbon dioxide and water
C	lactic acid	pyruvate	carbon dioxide and water
D	carbon dioxide and water	pyruvate	lactic acid

8. The apparatus shown below was used in an investigation of respiration in yeast.

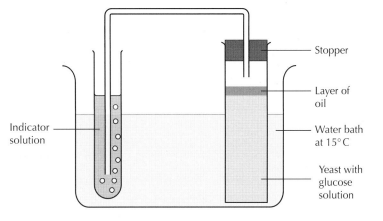

Which change to the apparatus would cause a **decrease** in the respiration rate of yeast?

A   Leaving out the oil layer

B   Diluting the glucose solution

C   Increasing the water bath temperature to 20 °C

D   Using cotton wool instead of a rubber stopper.

9. Which of the following is **not true** of meristem cells?

Meristem cells

A   can undergo cell division

B   have a specialised structure

C   contribute to the growth of plants

D   have potential to become any type of plant cell.

10. A homozygous black-coated male mouse was crossed with a homozygous brown-coated female.

All the F_1 mice were black.

The F_1 mice were allowed to mate, and the F_2 generation contained both black and brown mice.

What evidence is there that the allele for black coat is dominant to the allele for brown coat?

A   Only one of the original parents was black

B   The original male parent was black

C   All of the F_1 were black

D   Some of the F_2 were black.

11. In a breeding experiment with *Drosophila*, homozygous normal winged flies were crossed with homozygous vestigial winged flies. All of the F_1 were normal winged.

If flies from the F_1 were crossed, what percentage of their offspring would be expected to have normal wings?

A   25%

B   50%

C   75%

D   100%.

12. The diagram below shows a vertical section through a flower.

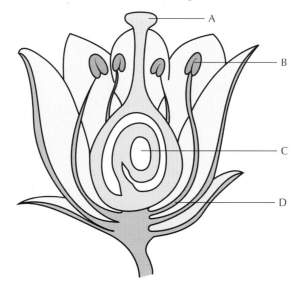

Which part produces male gametes?

13. The plant tissue that carries sugar from the leaves to the roots is the

A   mesophyll

B   xylem

C   phloem

D   epidermis.

14. The diagram below shows a single villus from the small intestine of a mammal.

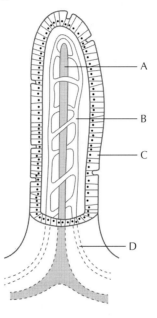

Which part is the lacteal?

15. Which line in the table below identifies correctly examples of biotic and abiotic factors affecting biodiversity?

	Biotic	*Abiotic*
A	temperature	grazing
B	pH	temperature
C	grazing	predation
D	predation	pH

16. The diagram below represents a pyramid of biomass.

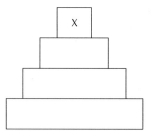

The block at X best represents the total biomass of

A producers

B decomposers

C predators

D prey.

17. Various aspects of a river were sampled at five points. The results are shown in the table below.

Aspect sampled	Sampling points				
	1	2	3	4	5
Mayfly nymph number	89	15	0	0	0
Midge larvae numbers	0	1	2	175	24
Oxygen concentration (% of maximum)	85	85	75	30	63
pH level	5.5	6.0	6.4	7.3	8.0

Based on the results in the table, which of the following conclusions is valid?

A High oxygen concentration limits the numbers of midge larvae

B pH level is proportional to oxygen concentration

C Midge larvae do not survive in water with low oxygen concentration

D Mayfly numbers depend on oxygen concentration alone.

18. The following stages are involved in speciation.

    1   Natural selection

    2   Isolation

    3   Mutation

In which order do these occur?

A   2→3→1

B   1→2→3

C   2→1→3

D   3→2→1.

19. The graph below shows the increase in the human population between the years 1400 and 2000.

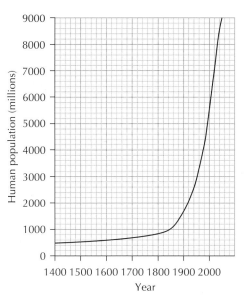

What was the percentage increase in the population between 1850 and 1950?

A   60%

B   200%

C   250%

D   50%.

20. A batch of cress seeds of the same variety were planted out into three containers, as shown below. The containers were well watered then placed together in a bright evenly-lit room.

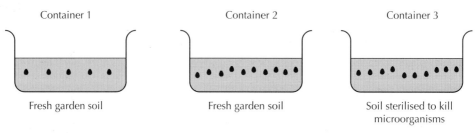

The diagrams below show the appearance of the containers after three days.

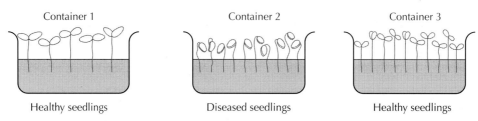

Which line in the table below correctly identifies the factor(s) involved in the diseased state of the seedlings in container 2?

	Factors		
	sowing density	microorganisms in soil	light intensity
A	✔	✔	✔
B	✔	✘	✘
C	✘	✔	✘
D	✔	✔	✘

Key

✔ Factor involved
✘ Factor not involved

N5 Biology

Practice Papers for SQA Exams   Section 2 – Questions

Fill in these boxes and read what is printed below.

Full name of centre

Town

Forename(s)

Surname

Try to answer ALL of the questions in the time allowed.

You have 2 hours to complete this paper.

Write your answers in the spaces provided, including all of your working.

Scotland's leading educational publishers

SECTION 2

1. Thin pieces of onion epidermis were immersed in solutions, as shown in the diagram below, and left for one hour.

Water

Thin piece of onion epidermis

A

Concentrated sugar solution

B

(a) The diagram below shows the appearance of an onion cell from dish A after one hour.

Complete the diagram to show the predicted appearance of a cell from dish B after this time.

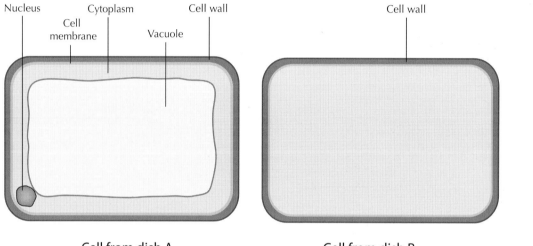

Nucleus   Cytoplasm   Cell wall

Cell membrane

Vacuole

Cell wall

Cell from dish A   Cell from dish B

2

(b) Give the term used to describe the state of a cell, such as that from dish A, which has been immersed in pure water for one hour.

_____

1

(c) (i) Name the process that has led to the different appearances of the onion cells in dishes A and B.

_____

1

(ii) The process responsible for these changes is described as being passive. Give the meaning of the term passive in this example.

_____

_____

1

(d) Complete the following sentence by <u>underlining</u> the correct option in each choice bracket.

Onion epidermis is a(n) $\left\{\begin{array}{l}\text{organ} \\ \text{tissue}\end{array}\right\}$ which is made up of cells carrying out a

$\left\{\begin{array}{l}\text{similar} \\ \text{different}\end{array}\right\}$ function.

1

Total marks 6

2. The diagram below represents cells from a region of cell division in a young plant root.

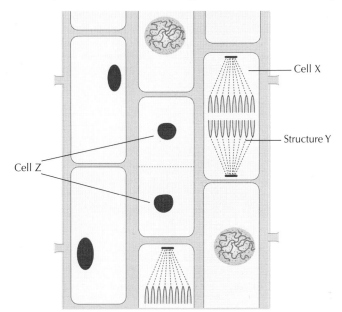

Cell X

Structure Y

Cell Z

(a) Describe the stage of mitosis shown in cell **X**.

_____

_____

1

(b) Name the structure labelled **Y**.

_____

1

(c) Complete the sentences below by <u>underlining</u> the correct option in each of the choice brackets.

The two nuclei in cell **Z** are genetically $\left\{\begin{array}{l}\text{different} \\ \text{identical}\end{array}\right\}$ to each other, and each has the

$\left\{\begin{array}{l}\text{haploid} \\ \text{diploid}\end{array}\right\}$ number of chromosomes. The two cells that are forming will be

$\left\{\begin{array}{l}\text{specialised} \\ \text{unspecialised}\end{array}\right\}$.

2

Total marks 4

3. The diagram below shows a stage of protein synthesis in which messenger RNA (mRNA) is formed in the nucleus of a cell.

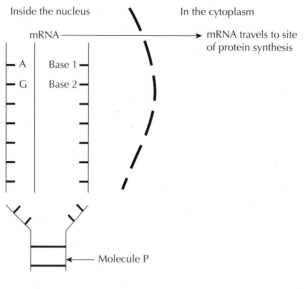

(a) Name molecule P.

_____

1

(b) Identify the bases 1, 2.

Base 1 _____

Base 2 _____

2

(c) Once complete, the mRNA molecule leaves the nucleus and enters the cytoplasm.

Identify the cell structures to which the mRNA travels and where protein synthesis takes place.

_____

1

(d) Describe the feature of the mRNA molecule that ensures that the correct protein is synthesised.

_____

_____

1

(e) Give **one** function of proteins in cells.

_____

1

Total marks 6

4. In an investigation of fermentation, 20 cm³ of a yeast suspension was added to 50 cm³ of grape juice and the carbon dioxide gas produced was collected and measured, as shown in the diagram below.

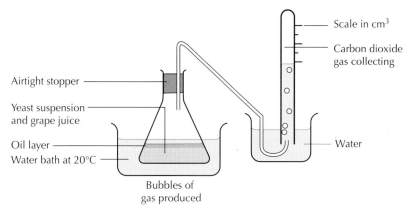

The rate of fermentation was calculated every 2 days for 10 days. The results are shown in the table below.

Day	Rate of fermentation (cm³ carbon dioxide produced per hour)
0	0
2	15
4	25
6	30
8	12
10	2

(a) On the grid below plot a line graph to show the rate of fermentation against time.

(A spare grid, if required, can be found on page 56.)

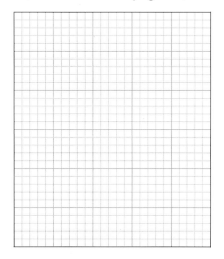

2

(b) Calculate the simplest whole number ratio of volume of carbon dioxide produced per hour after 2 days to that produced after 8 days.
Space for calculations

$$\underline{\qquad} : \underline{\qquad}$$
2 days   8 days

1

(c) Suggest a reason for the reduction in rate of fermentation after day 6.

_____

_____

1

(d) Suggest an improvement to the method described that would allow the investigation to be repeated more accurately.

_____

_____

1

(e) The list shows various factors that could affect the rate of respiration.

temperature   concentration of grape juice   concentration of yeast suspension

Choose a factor and describe how the apparatus could be used to investigate its effect on the rate of fermentation.

Factor chosen _____

Description _____

_____

1

Total marks   6

5.   The diagram below shows the ends of two neurons J and M, the gaps between them and a relay neuron K within the spinal cord in the central nervous system of a mammal.

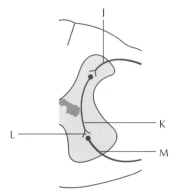

(a) Describe how a nervous message is passed along a neuron such as J.

_____   1

(b) Describe how a nervous message arriving at the end of neuron K is able to cross the gap L.

_____

_____   1

(c) Name gap L.

_____   1

(d) Give **one** characteristic of a reflex action and explain the advantage it provides for mammals.

Characteristic _____   1

Advantage _____   1

Total marks 5

6. The bar chart below shows variation in the length of seeds harvested from a broad bean plant.

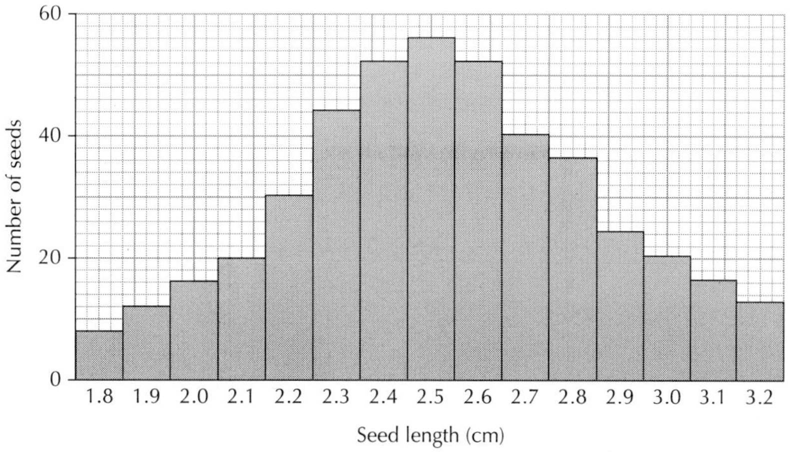

(a) Calculate the difference between the shortest and longest seeds in the sample.

Space for calculations

_____ cm   1

(b) Give evidence to support the statement that the seed length shows continuous variation.

_____

_____   1

MARKS
Do not write in this margin

(c) Give **one** example of a characteristic from a **named** animal or plant species that shows discrete variation.

Named species ______________________

Characteristic ______________________ 1

Total marks 3

7. The diagram below shows the heart and an outline of the circulatory system of a human.

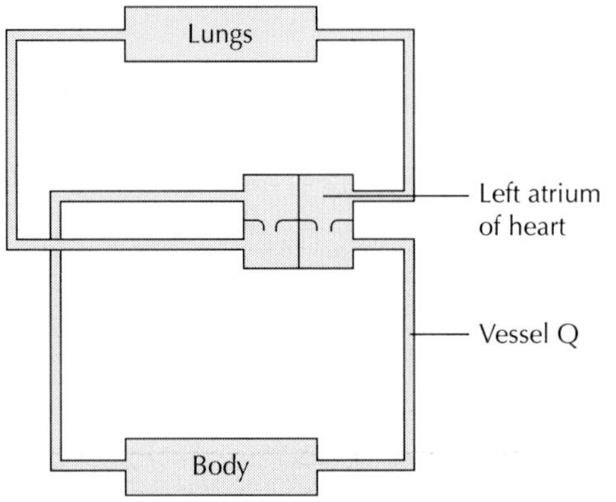

(a) **On the diagram**:

(i) Use the letter P to label the pulmonary artery. 1

(ii) Draw an arrow on vessel Q to show the direction of blood flow. 1

(b) Name the structures found in the heart and veins that prevent the backflow of blood.

______________________ 1

(c) Give **one** difference between arteries and veins.

______________________ 1

(d) Describe how red blood cells are adapted to take up and transport oxygen.

____

____

____

____

______________________ 2

Total marks 6

8. The graph below shows the average transpiration rate of barley plants in an open field over a 24-hour period during summer in Scotland.

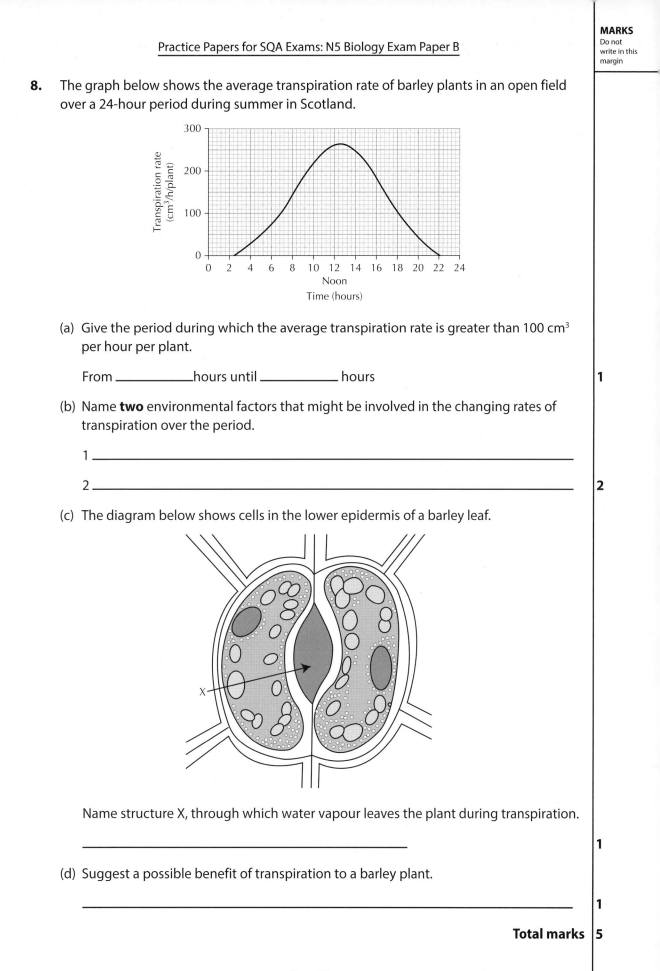

(a) Give the period during which the average transpiration rate is greater than 100 cm^3 per hour per plant.

From _____ hours until _____ hours

1

(b) Name **two** environmental factors that might be involved in the changing rates of transpiration over the period.

1 _____

2 _____

2

(c) The diagram below shows cells in the lower epidermis of a barley leaf.

Name structure X, through which water vapour leaves the plant during transpiration.

_____

1

(d) Suggest a possible benefit of transpiration to a barley plant.

_____

1

Total marks **5**

9. The charts below show the occurrence of five species of plants in samples taken from an area of grassland and from a path passing through it.

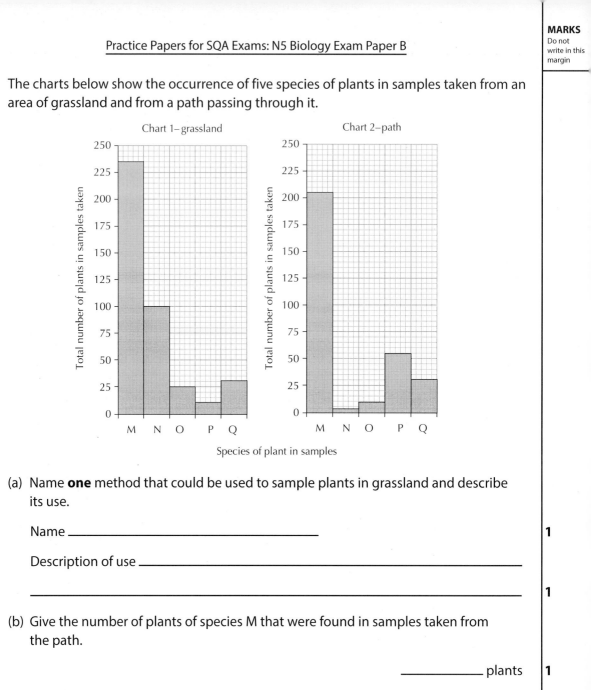

Chart 1– grassland

Chart 2–path

Species of plant in samples

(a) Name **one** method that could be used to sample plants in grassland and describe its use.

Name _____ **1**

Description of use _____

_____ **1**

(b) Give the number of plants of species M that were found in samples taken from the path.

_____ plants **1**

(c) Describe the effects on the numbers of species O and P of being walked over by people using the path.

Species O _____ **1**

Species P _____ **1**

(d) Give the species that is least affected by being walked over.

Species _____ **1**

Total marks **6**

MARKS Do not write in this margin

10. The diagram below shows part of the nitrogen cycle.

The letters X, Y and Z represent different types of bacteria involved in the cycle.

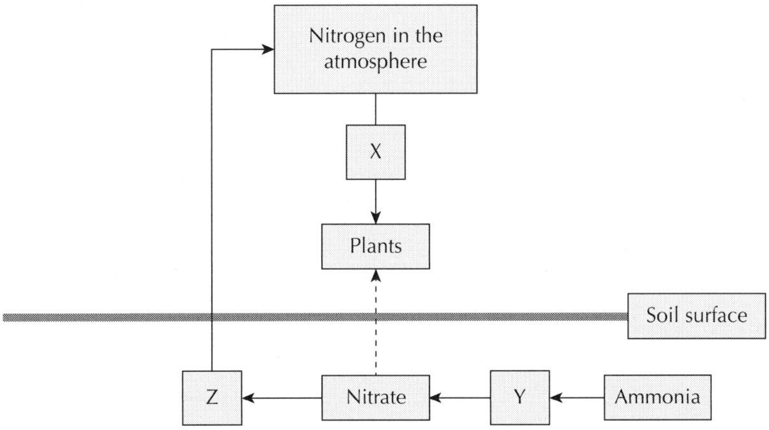

(a) Choose **one** letter, name the type of bacteria present and describe their role in the nitrogen cycle.

Letter ____________

Name ____________________ **1**

Role in nitrogen cycle ____

____ **1**

(b) Name **one** type of substance that is produced by plants using nitrate absorbed in the nitrogen cycle.

____ **1**

(c) Name the nitrate-containing substances that are added to soil by farmers to increase the yield of their crops.

____ **1**

Total marks 4

11. (a) The table below refers to mutation.

Decide if each statement in the table is true or false and tick (✔) the appropriate box.

Statement	***True***	***False***
Mutation is a non-random event.		
Mutation can confer an advantage to an organism.		
Mutation is the only source of new alleles.		

2

MARKS Do not write in this margin

(b) Describe how natural selection is involved in the evolution of new species. 3

Total marks 5

12. Lichens live on the surfaces of walls and trees, and are sensitive to sulfur dioxide, a gas linked with air pollution.

The graph below shows the results of a study in which the percentage of surfaces that were covered by lichens along a line from the centre of a large city that had air polluted by sulfur dioxide was estimated.

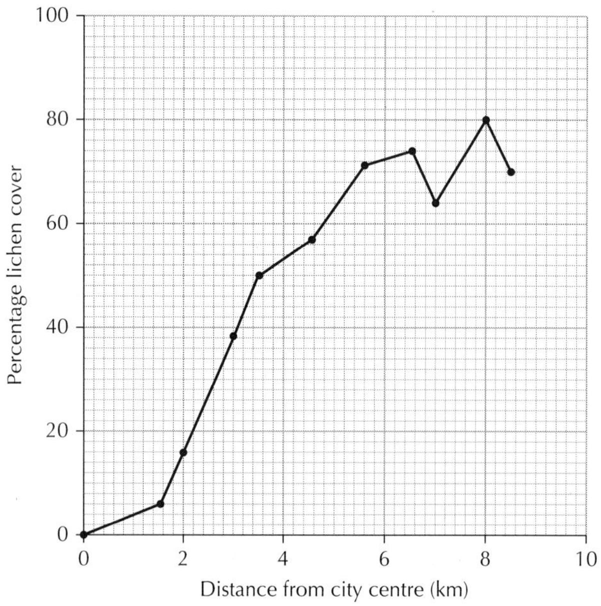

(a) Lichens can be used as indicators of air pollution.

Describe how this statement is supported by the data shown in the graph. 1

(b) At what distance from the city centre was the air pollution the lowest as indicated by percentage lichen cover?

______ km 1

(c) As well as sulfur dioxide, polluted air often contains tiny black soot particles.

Predict how these particles would affect the rate of photosynthesis in plants growing in polluted air. Explain your answer.

Prediction _____ **1**

Explanation _____

_____ **1**

Total marks **4**

[END OF QUESTION PAPER]

ADDITIONAL GRAPH PAPER

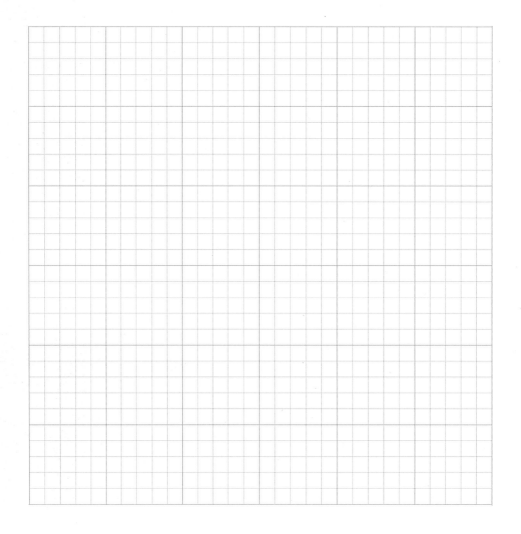

Practice Exam C

SECTION 1 ANSWER GRID

Mark the correct answer as shown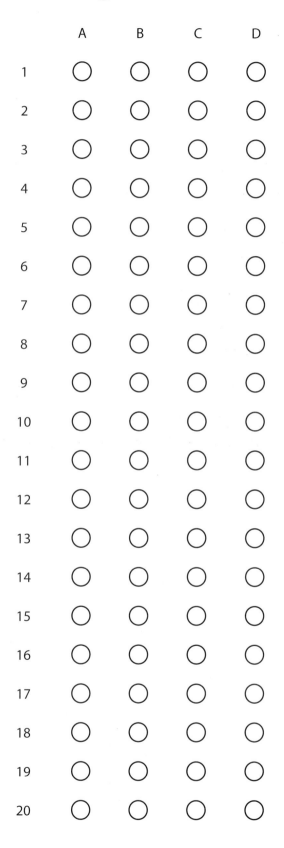

	A	B	C	D
1	○	○	○	○
2	○	○	○	○
3	○	○	○	○
4	○	○	○	○
5	○	○	○	○
6	○	○	○	○
7	○	○	○	○
8	○	○	○	○
9	○	○	○	○
10	○	○	○	○
11	○	○	○	○
12	○	○	○	○
13	○	○	○	○
14	○	○	○	○
15	○	○	○	○
16	○	○	○	○
17	○	○	○	○
18	○	○	○	○
19	○	○	○	○
20	○	○	○	○

N5 Biology

Practice Papers for SQA Exams   Section 1 – Questions

Fill in these boxes and read what is printed below.

Full name of centre   Town

Forename(s)   Surname

Try to answer ALL of the questions in the time allowed.

You have 2 hours to complete this paper.

Write your answers in the spaces provided, including all of your working.

Scotland's leading educational publishers

SECTION 1

1. Red blood cells were placed into a salt solution more concentrated than blood plasma.

   Which word best describes the predicted appearance of the cells after a few seconds in this solution?

   A Burst

   B Plasmolysed

   C Turgid

   D Shrunken.

2. The diagram below shows molecules present in the cell membrane.

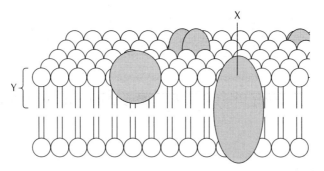

   Which line in the table identifies correctly molecules X and Y?

	Molecule X	Molecule Y
A	protein	phospholipid
B	protein	phosphate
C	phospholipid	protein
D	phospholipid	phosphate

3. The diagram below shows a stage in the formation of a molecule of messenger RNA (mRNA).

Which line in the table below shows letters that identify correctly Bases 1 and 2?

	Base 1	Base 2
A	C	A
B	G	A
C	C	T
D	G	T

4. The graph below shows the effect of pH on the activity of four human digestive enzymes.

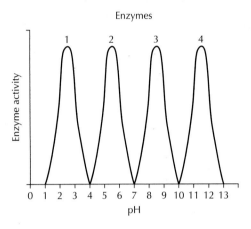

Which enzyme(s) work best in acid pH?

A   1 only

B   1 and 2

C   3 and 4

D   4 only.

5. The descriptions below refer to events in mitosis.

1   Spindle forms

2   Chromatids separate

3   Chromosomes move to equator

4   Nuclei form

Which is the correct order of these events?

A   4→3→2→1

B   1→3→2→4

C   4→2→3→1

D   1→2→3→4.

6. The diagram below shows two events in the first stage of photosynthesis in a leaf cell.

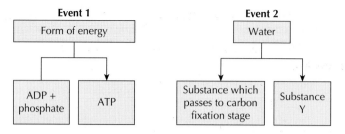

Which line in the table below identifies correctly the form of energy in event 1 and substance Y?

	Form of energy	Substance Y
A	light	hydrogen
B	chemical	oxygen
C	light	oxygen
D	chemical	hydrogen

7. The graph below shows the effect of increasing light intensity on the rate of photosynthesis at different temperatures and carbon dioxide concentrations.

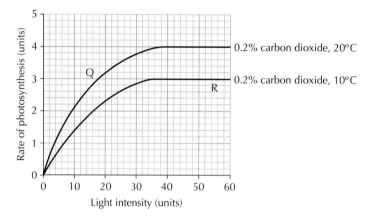

Which line in the table shows correctly the factors that are limiting photosynthesis at points Q and R on the graph?

	Q	R
A	light intensity	temperature
B	carbon dioxide concentration	temperature
C	light intensity	carbon dioxide concentration
D	temperature	light intensity

8. The flow chart below shows information about the regulation of blood glucose in humans.

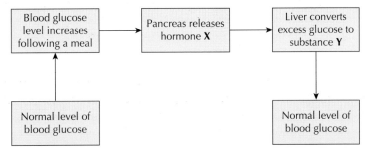

Which line in the table below identifies correctly hormone **X** and substance **Y**?

	Hormone X	Substance Y
A	insulin	starch
B	glucagon	glycogen
C	insulin	glycogen
D	glucagon	starch

9. The diagram below shows a vertical section through a flower of the pea family.

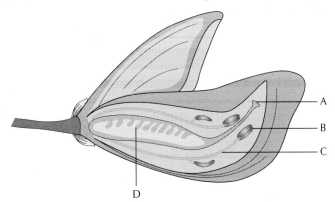

In which structure are female gametes produced?

10. A pea plant with yellow seeds was crossed with a pea plant with green seeds. All of the F_1 plants produced had yellow seeds.

The genotype of the parent plant with green seeds could be described as

A heterozygous and recessive

B homozygous and dominant

C heterozygous and dominant

D homozygous and recessive.

Questions 11 and 12 refer to the diagram below, which shows a cross-section through a young plant stem and a cell from a part of the stem.

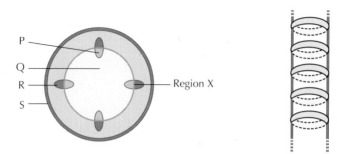

11. In which part of the cross-section would the cell shown be found?

A P

B Q

C R

D S.

12. Cells in region X undergo mitosis.

What name is given to region X?

A Stem cell

B Mesophyll

C Meristem

D Anther.

13. The diagram below shows part of the human digestive system.

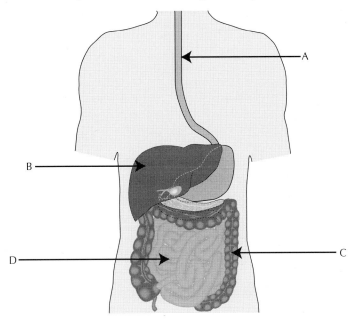

In which region of the diagram would villi be found?

14. Which line in the table below correctly identifies the location of the start and the completion of the respiration pathways shown?

| | Fermentation pathway | | Aerobic pathway | |
	starts in	completed in	starts in	completed in
A	mitochondria	cytoplasm	mitochondria	cytoplasm
B	mitochondria	mitochondria	mitochondria	cytoplasm
C	cytoplasm	cytoplasm	cytoplasm	mitochondria
D	cytoplasm	mitochondria	cytoplasm	mitochondria

15. Which term describes all the organisms living in an area and the non-living factors with which the organisms interact?

A   Habitat

B   Ecosystem

C   Biome

D   Niche.

16. The diagram below shows a pyramid of numbers representing a food chain.

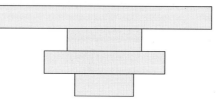

Which of the following food chains could be represented by this pyramid?

A   oak tree → moth caterpillar → blue tit → feather mite (a parasite)

B   oak tree → greenfly → ladybird → blue tit (predator)

C   heather → moth caterpillar → meadow pipit → merlin (a predator)

D   heather → moth caterpillar → meadow pipit → feather mite (a parasite).

17. Some organisms living in seas off the east coast of Scotland are shown in the food web below.

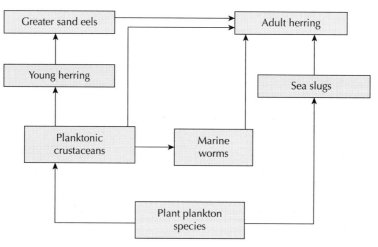

Which line in the table below shows correctly pairs of organisms that are involved in the types of competition shown?

	Type of competition	
	interspecific	**intraspecific**
A	planktonic crustaceans and sea slugs	young and adult herring
B	young and adult herring	greater sand eels and planktonic crustaceans
C	young and adult herring	marine worms and sea slugs
D	planktonic crustaceans and sea slugs	two species of plant plankton

18. In an investigation, the average numbers of individuals of two forms of the peppered moth in city woodland were estimated every year over a five-year period.

The results are shown on the bar chart below.

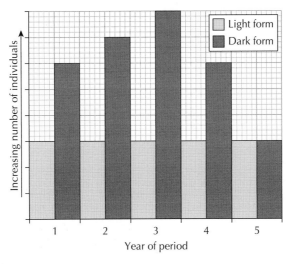

Between which two years of the period did the greatest change in the ratio of light to dark moths occur?

A   1 and 2

B   2 and 3

C   3 and 4

D   4 and 5.

19. An indirect effect of fertiliser leaching from cereal crop fields into fresh water is reduction in oxygen levels in the water.

Which group of organisms deoxygenates the water?

A   Algae

B   Bacteria

C   Cereal crops

D   Freshwater plants.

20. In an investigation, the concentration of a pesticide in the bodies of four individual birds found dead in a farmland area was measured. Two of the birds were predators, and two were prey species.

The results are shown in the table below.

Bird species	Predator or prey species	Concentration of pesticide (units per gram of muscle)
wood pigeon	prey	4
skylark	prey	2
sparrowhawk	predator	26
barn owl	predator	16

What is the difference between the average units of pesticide per gram of muscle in the prey species compared to the average in the predator species?

A   12

B   18

C   36

D   39.

N5 Biology

Practice Papers for SQA Exams   Section 2 – Questions

Fill in these boxes and read what is printed below.

Full name of centre   Town

Forename(s)   Surname

Try to answer ALL of the questions in the time allowed.

You have 2 hours to complete this paper.

Write your answers in the spaces provided, including all of your working.

Scotland's leading educational publishers

SECTION 2

1. The diagram below represents a cell from a green plant.

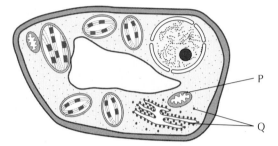

(a) Give evidence from the diagram that suggests that this cell can carry out photosynthesis.

_____ 1

(b) Give the function of structure P.

_____ 1

(c) Name structures Q.

_____ 1

(d) Give **one** structural difference that would be expected between this cell and a fungal cell.

_____ 1

Total marks 4

2. The diagram below shows the transport of molecule S through a cell membrane.

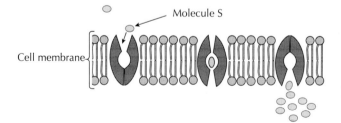

(a) Name the method shown in the diagram by which molecule S is being moved across the membrane. Give **one** reason for your answer.

Method _____ 1

Reason _____ 1

(b) In an investigation, small pieces of tissue of known mass were taken from a water plant submerged in pond water. They were placed into different concentrations of sucrose solution for one hour. After this time, the mass of each piece of tissue was re-measured and expressed as a percentage of its original volume.

The results are shown in the table below.

Concentration of sucrose solution (grams per litre)	Final mass of tissue (% of its mass in pond water)
0	100.0
5	98.5
10	95.0
15	92.5
20	90.5
25	90.0

(i)   On the grid below, complete the vertical axis and plot a line graph to show the effect of sucrose concentration on the mass of the water plant tissue. (A spare grid, if required, can be found on page 82)

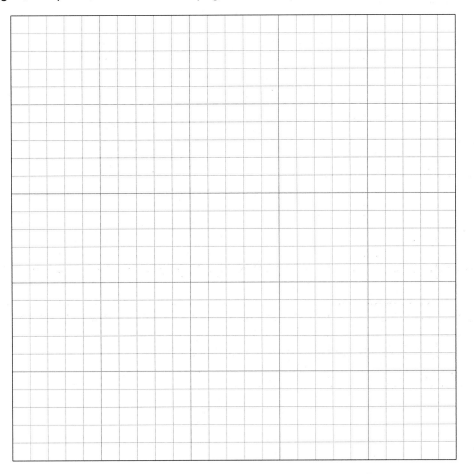

2

MARKS Do not write in this margin

(ii) Name the process that causes the mass changes in the water plant tissue.

____________________ 1

(iii) Using the information available in the table, predict the final mass of a piece of water plant tissue with a starting mass of 2.0 g after it has been immersed in a 25% sucrose solution for one hour.

Final mass = ________ g 1

Total marks 6

3. The diagram below shows the genetic modification of a bacterial cell by the transfer of a human gene.

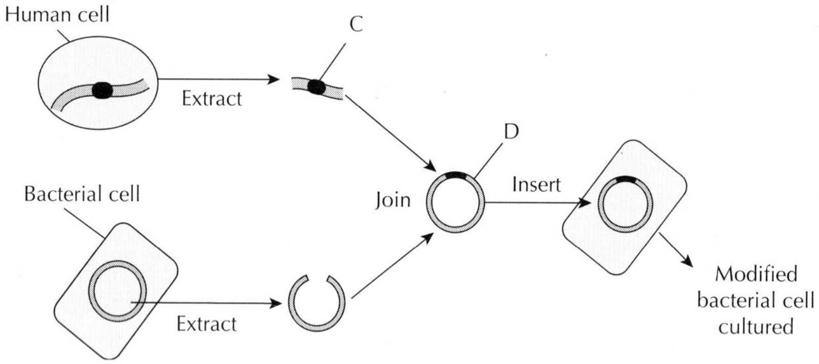

(a) Name the substance of which the human gene C is composed.

____________________ 1

(b) Identify structure D.

____________________ 1

(c) The modified bacteria can be cultured to produce a large population.

Cell culture requires the following:

Aseptic techniques **An appropriate medium** **Control of temperature and pH**

Choose **one** of these and explain its importance in cell culture.

Choice ____________________

Importance ____________________

____________________ 1

(d) Give **one** example of a substance produced by the expression of a human gene that has been obtained by this method.

_____ 1

Total marks 4

4. When mammalian muscle tissue contracts, it decreases in length.

The **diagram** below shows the procedure involved in an investigation into the effect of different solutions on the lengths of pieces of mammalian muscle tissue. Each piece of muscle tissue was measured before and after five minutes of immersion in the solutions.

The results are shown in the **table** below.

Muscle tissue	Solution	Length of muscle tissue (mm)			Percentage difference in length (%)
		at start	after five minutes	difference in length	
A	1% glucose	45	45	0	0
B	1% ATP	50	46	4	
C	distilled water	48	48	0	0

(a) **Complete the table** by calculating the percentage decrease in length of muscle tissue B.

_____% 1

(b) Explain why glucose has no effect on muscle tissue A, whereas ATP causes muscle tissue B to contract.

_____

_____ 2

MARKS Do not write in this margin

(c) Describe why muscle tissue C was included in the experimental design.

____

____ 1

(d) State what is meant by the term **tissue** in this example.

____ 1

Total marks 5

5. The diagram below shows some structures involved in an example of a rapid reflex action in humans.

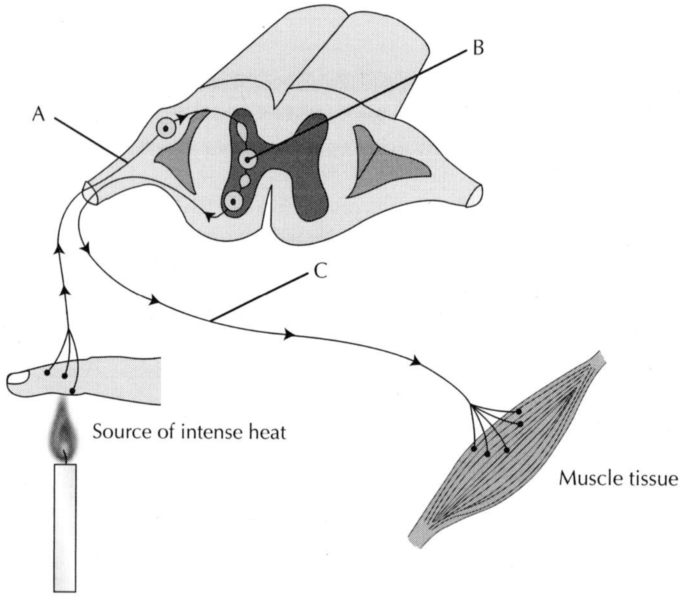
B
A
C
Source of intense heat
Muscle tissue

(a) Neurons A, B and C form the reflex arc.

Name each of these neurons.

A ______________________________

B ______________________________

C ______________________________ 2

(b) Identify the stimulus and describe the expected response in this example.

Stimulus ______________________________ 1

Description of response ______________________________

____ 1

(c) Explain the importance of rapid reflex actions in general.

_____

_____ 1

Total marks 5

6. Garden pea plants that carry the allele **T** have a tall phenotype.

Plants with the genotype **tt** are dwarf.

20 seeds of a tall variety and 20 seeds of a dwarf variety were germinated and grown for 15 weeks in a greenhouse. After this time the height of each plant was measured, and the results are shown in the charts below.

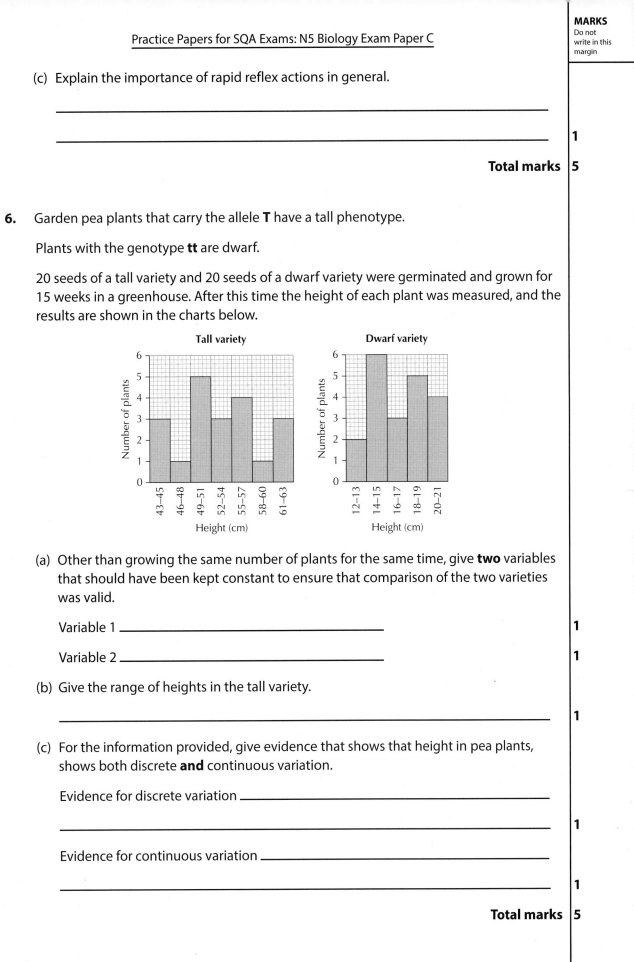

(a) Other than growing the same number of plants for the same time, give **two** variables that should have been kept constant to ensure that comparison of the two varieties was valid.

Variable 1 _____ 1

Variable 2 _____ 1

(b) Give the range of heights in the tall variety.

_____ 1

(c) For the information provided, give evidence that shows that height in pea plants, shows both discrete **and** continuous variation.

Evidence for discrete variation _____

_____ 1

Evidence for continuous variation _____

_____ 1

Total marks 5

7. (a) The diagram below shows an external view of the human heart.

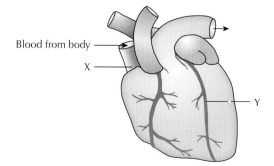

Blood from body —
X —

— Y

(i) Identify blood vessels X and Y.

X _____ **1**

Y _____ **1**

(ii) Decide if each of the statements about blood vessels in the grid below is true or false and tick (✔) the correct box.

If the statement is false write the correct word in the box to replace the word underlined in the statement.

Statement	True	False	Correction
Arteries carry blood <u>from</u> the heart.			
<u>Veins</u> exchange materials with the tissues.			
<u>Capillaries</u> have valves.			

2

(b) The graph below shows the effect of carbon dioxide concentration in the air on the volume of air inhaled into the lungs of an individual at rest.

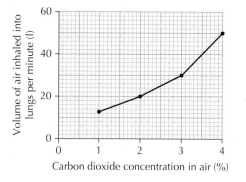

(i)   Calculate the volume of carbon dioxide entering the individual's lungs each minute when the volume of air inhaled is 20 litres per minute.

_____ litres **1**

(ii) Calculate the increase in volume of air entering the lungs per minute when the concentration of carbon dioxide in the air increases from 1% to 4%.

_____ litres **1**

Total marks **6**

8.   In an investigation into the effects of temperature on rate of transpiration in a leafy seedling, the apparatus below was set up.

- Leafy seedling
- Layer of oil
- Glass jar
- Water
- Top pan balance

Transpiration rate was measured at different temperatures. The results are shown in the table below.

Temperature (°C)	Transpiration rate (grams of water per cm² of leaf per minute)
10	0.2
15	0.3
20	0.4
25	0.5

(a) Identify the observations or measurements that would have to be made to obtain the values for rate of transpiration shown in the table.

_____

_____

_____ **3**

(b) The following factors can affect transpiration rate in plants.

Light intensity   **Atmospheric humidity**   **Air movements**

Choose **one** of these factors and describe how the apparatus above could be modified to investigate this factor.

Factor _____

Description _____

_____

2

Total marks 5

9. The pie chart below shows one estimate of the percentage of the Earth's land area occupied by different biomes.

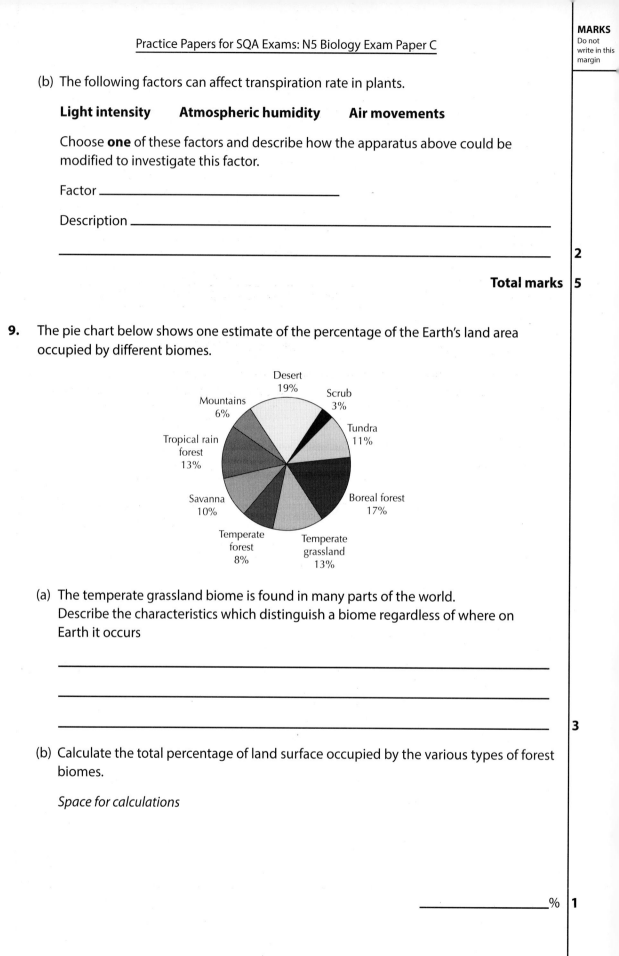

(a) The temperate grassland biome is found in many parts of the world. Describe the characteristics which distinguish a biome regardless of where on Earth it occurs

_____

_____

_____

3

(b) Calculate the total percentage of land surface occupied by the various types of forest biomes.

Space for calculations

_____% 1

(c) Within biomes, organisms live in communities, and each species occupies its own niche.

Describe what is meant by the term niche.

_____

_____ **1**

Total marks | **5**

10. In an investigation to compare the populations of a species of ground beetle living on the soil surface in two different areas of grassland, sampling was carried out using pitfall traps.

(a) Give **two** precautions that would have to be taken to ensure that the sampling method allowed valid **comparison** of the two areas.

1 _____

2 _____ **2**

(b) Describe a source of error that can arise when using pitfall traps.

_____ **1**

(c) During the investigation, a number of abiotic factors related to the soil were also measured.

Name **one** abiotic factor that is related to soil and describe how it could be measured.

Abiotic factor _____ **1**

Method of measurement _____

_____ **1**

Total marks | **5**

11. On the Galapagos Islands of the Pacific Ocean, speciation has produced a group of similar finch species, as shown in the diagram below. The group arose from a single ancestor species, which reached the islands from the South American mainland millions of years ago.

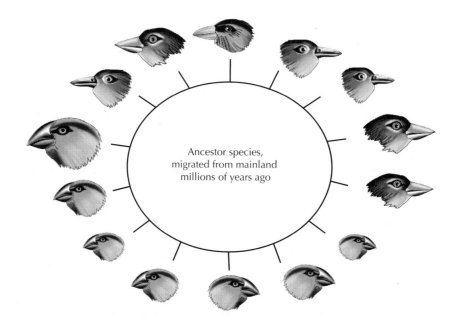

Ancestor species, migrated from mainland millions of years ago

(a) The list below shows processes involved in speciation.

mutation   **isolation**   **natural selection**

Describe how these processes have led to the production of the group of finch species in the diagram above.

_____

_____

_____

_____

_____ **3**

(b) Give the term applied to mutations that confer neither advantage nor disadvantage.

_____ **1**

Total marks **4**

12. The diagram below shows part of the nitrogen cycle in a field in which a cereal crop was grown.

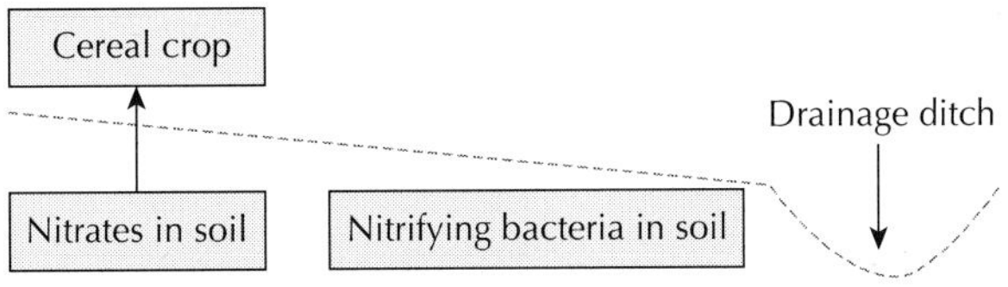

```
        ┌──────────────┐
        │ Cereal crop  │
        └──────────────┘
            ▲                              Drainage ditch
            │
   ┌──────────────┐  ┌──────────────────────────┐
   │Nitrates in soil│  │Nitrifying bacteria in soil│      ↓
   └──────────────┘  └──────────────────────────┘
```

(a) Describe the role of nitrifying bacteria in soil.

_____   **1**

(b) Other than the action of denitrifying bacteria, give **two** ways in which nitrogen could be lost from the nitrogen cycle in this field.

1 _____   **1**

2 _____   **1**

(c) Farmers replace nitrogen lost from their soils.

(i) State how nitrogen can be replaced as part of intensive farming practices.

_____   **1**

(ii) Nitrogen can be replaced as part of organic farming practices using plants such as clover, which have root-nodule bacteria.

Explain how planting clover can replace lost nitrogen.

_____

_____   **1**

(d) Describe **one** way in which the environmental impact of cereal production by intensive farming could be reduced.

_____   **1**

Total marks **6**

[END OF QUESTION PAPER]

ADDITIONAL GRAPH PAPER

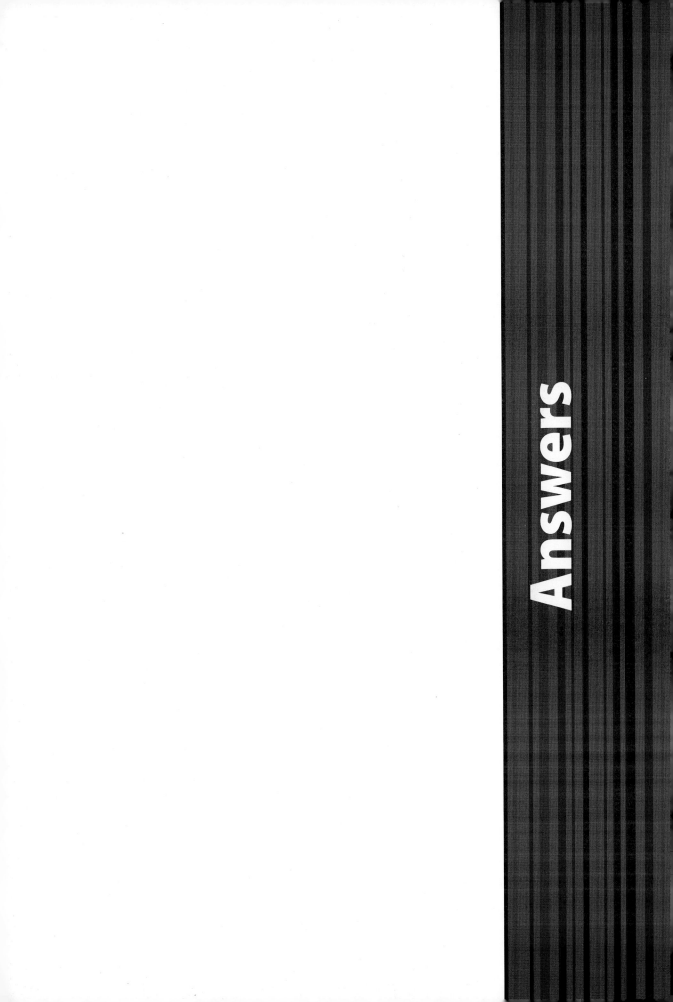

Answers

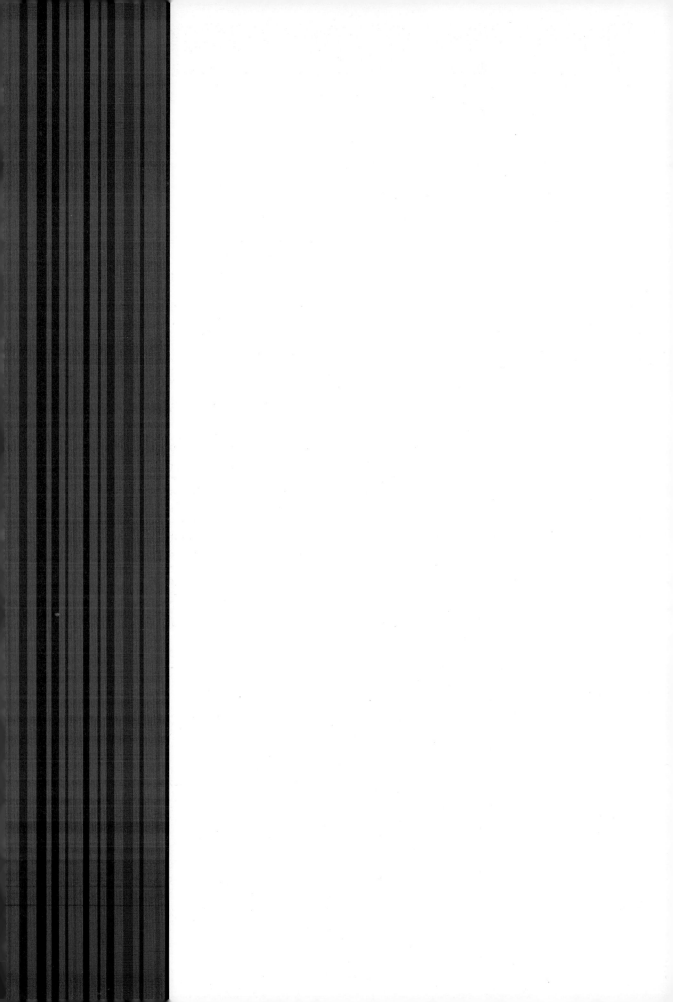

Answers to Practice Exams

Practice Exam A

Section 1

Question	Response	Mark	Top Tips
1.	B	1	You must be able to identify cell structures from diagrams and know their functions.
2.	C	1	Find the number of cells and then divide it by the total number of cells – multiply the answer by 100. (15/50) x 100 = 30%
3.	B	1	Tricky – you need to go through each option – it will take a bit of time and making some sketches might help. You can draw on the question paper!
4.	A	1	You need to know the three features of active transport – against concentration gradient, involves proteins, needs energy/ATP.
5.	D	1	Language is crucial – you need to know the terms chromatid and spindle fibre, and their roles in mitosis.
6.	B	1	DNA looks like a twisted ladder – the rungs are the bases that carry the genetic code.
7.	D	1	Bacterial chromosomes are usually long and coiled up, but plasmids look neat and circular.
8.	D	1	You need to learn the levels of organisation in biology – cell, tissue, organ, system, organism.
9.	C	1	Watch for the **bold** in the question – tick off the true options as you work through.
10.	A	1	This is a standard type of brain diagram – you must be able to identify where particular functions occur.
11.	C	1	The key here is reading the question – the word **respond** is crucial – candidates could be wrongly attracted by pancreas, which **produces** insulin.
12.	B	1	You need to appreciate that gametes are the only haploid cells mentioned in National 5 Biology.
13.	C	1	Just like maths – A = B x C so B must be A divided by C. Calculator almost essential! Remember, 4 litres = 4000 cm^3
14.	B	1	You just need to learn these words – why not make yourself a set of flash cards? Put the word on one side and the meaning on the other.

Question	Response	Mark	Top Tips
15.	D	1	The **bold** is vital, and again it is the term **community** that needs to be learned.
16.	D	1	The word **bio**tic sounds like **bio**logy for a good reason – you are looking for **living** factors.
17.	C	1	A bit tricky but if 90% is lost, 10% is kept. Writing the figures under the organisms' names in the chain will help keep you right.
18.	A	1	Tricky – take each option in turn. B and C are clearly wrong but D looks attractive. Remember that plants need nitrates and make their own amino acids and proteins.
19.	A	1	It is vital to remember that the 0 value counts – so the total number of limpets is divided by the 9 quadrats.
20.	A	1	It is worth trying to sort out the difference between validity and reliability – it's tough because they do overlap a bit.

Practice Exam A

Section 2

Question			Expected response	Mark	Top Tips
1.	(a)		X lipid = **1** Y protein = **1**	2	You need to learn the appearance of the two molecules in diagrams.
	(b)		selectively down does not require **All 3 = 2, 2 or 1 = 1**	2	Remember that the concentration gradient is a bit like a physical slope – so up, down – with and against are good terms!
	(c)	(i)	place in a solution of lower water concentration than cell sap	1	Position of the cell membrane is vital in identification of cell condition.
	(c)	(ii)	plasmolysed	1	Remember **PS** – **P**lasmolysed in **S**trong solution.
2.	(a)		P R Q	1	The words **building up** in the stem of the question are crucial to answering. **S**ynthesis **s**tarts with **s**mall molecules.

Question			Expected response	Mark	Top Tips
	(b)		active site	1	The shape of the active site allows reaction with specific substrate molecules.
	(c)		active site shape altered/ denatured = **1** cannot bind to substrate = **1**	2	Temperature is critical in biology – proteins don't like heat!
3.	(a)		A = hydrogen B = ATP C = oxygen **All 3 = 2, 2 or 1 = 1**	2	This is a useful diagram – you could copy it and put in the missing information for your revision notes.
	(b)	(i)	no starch present = **1** CO_2 needed for photosynthesis = **1**	2	Starch storage is a sign that photosynthesis has happened, and excess sugar/glucose has been produced.
	(b)	(ii)	set up as leaf A but without substance to absorb CO_2	1	Controls allow comparison with results and show if an experimental variable is causing a result.
	(b)	(iii)	repeat experiment but remove glass tubes, cover one leaf to exclude light	1	This is a common question type – there are three parts to the standard answer. Repeat, hold original variable constant, alter new variable.
4.	(a)		scales and labels = **1** points and connection = **1**	2	Include zeros and highest values on even scales. Include units with labels. Plot with a sharp pencil. Connect plots with straight lines.
	(b)		carbon dioxide	1	Remember CO_2 is produced in fermentation as well as in aerobic respiration.
	(c)		measure volume of gas rather than counting bubbles	1	**Accurate** is the key word – this usually relates to the measurement method.
	(d)		rate would decrease = **1** enzymes work slowly in cool conditions = **1**	2	You must realise that fermentation is enzyme controlled.

Question			Expected response	Mark	Top Tips
5.	(a)		sensory neuron	1	There are three types of neuron to be known – sensory, relay and motor.
	(b)		synapse = **1** allow transfer of electrical impulses to the next neuron = **1**	2	Electrical impulses can only cross when the synapses are filled with chemical transmitter.
	(c)		protection from excess heat = **1** improved survival chances = **1**	2	The word *protection* is vital here, and the diagram in the question gives the clue to the type of damage avoided.
6.	(a)		J Rr K Rr L rr **All 3 = 2, 2 or 1 = 1**	2	It is worth adding the known alleles onto the diagram on the paper to make answering easier.
	(b)		N has allele R because he is a roller = **1** other allele could be either R or r = **1**	2	Doubt about offspring is because at least one parent is heterozygous.
7.	(a)		W xylem, water/minerals X phloem, sugar **All 4 = 3, 3 or 2 = 2, 1 = 1**	3	Just learn it but you could try the F sounds – *phloem for food*.
	(b)		lignin	1	**XL** – **X**ylem has **L**ignin.
8.	(a)		keep airway open	1	Just like hoses on vacuum cleaners – airways need support.
	(b)		• mucus is sticky • traps inhaled particles/pathogens • cilia drive mucus upwards • into mouth to be swallowed **Any 3 = 3, any 2 = 2, any 1 = 1**	3	The sticky conveyor belt idea will help here.
	(c)	(i)	age number of cigarettes smoked daily **both**	1	Look carefully for the factors that vary in the data.
	(c)	(ii)	200%	1	Use a clear plastic ruler to help with the graph reading and remember that doubling a number is a 100% increase.

	Question		Expected response	Mark	Top Tips
9.	(a)		species Q correctly adapted beak and habitat preference **both**	1	Spotting the link here is crucial – the table describes beak shape, and the diagrams show beak shape.
	(b)		different food = **1** different habitat = **1**	2	Interspecific competition occurs when the **same** resources in the **same** habitat are required by **two** species – competition is reduced when requirements are different.
	(c)		R P Q	1	What about trying **I'M** a **N**ew **S**pecies. **I**solation – **M**utation – **N**atural **S**election?
10.	(a)		quadrats drop randomly	1	The only plant-sampling technique in National 5 assessment is quadrats.
	(b)		3:1	1	Ensure that your ratio has only whole numbers.
	(c)		20 000	1	This is where the need to know the number of m^2 in a hectare given in the question comes in.
	(d)		light intensity = **1** shade of trees in woodland reduces photosynthesis at ground level = **1**	2	You need to visualise a wood compared with an open grassy area – light and shade should come to mind! There could be other answers too though.
11.	(a)		B C A **All 3 = 2, 2 or 1 = 1**	2	Why not copy the table and add in what each bacteria group does for your revision notes?
	(b)		protein/polypeptide/amino acid/ nucleic acid	1	Plants take up nitrates, use them to make amino acids, then synthesise these into proteins.
	(c)		decomposers	1	Not all decomposers are bacteria – fungi and some other organisms can also be involved.

Question			Expected response	Mark	Top Tips
12.	(a)		adds (aerobic) bacteria to water/ has nutrients which allow = 1 9 (aerobic) 0 bacteria to multiply = 1 (aerobic) bacteria use up oxygen = 1	3	The relationship between sewage and dissolved oxygen in water needs to be learned – it's a bit tricky, and the role of bacteria is crucial.
	(b)		increase in nitrate levels	1	Use a clear plastic ruler to add a line up from Q and R to make the question clearer.
	(c)		algae undergo photosynthesis, which produces oxygen	1	Using knowledge from other key areas is often required. Here it is about photosynthesis.
	(d)		all factors return to levels before addition of sewage	1	Compare the start of the graph to the end.

Practice Exam B

Section 1

Question	Response	Mark	Top Tips
1.	D	1	Here again you must be able to recognise cell structures from diagrams and have learned their functions.
2.	D	1	Count the cell lengths up the field of view and divide the number into 1000 micrometres.
3.	C	1	Candidates sometimes confuse **specific** and **optimum** – make sure you know the difference.
4.	B	1	The extraction order does not matter but the insertion order does!
5.	D	1	Crucial here to notice that increasing distance decreases light intensity.
6.	A	1	Think about energy forms. Light energy trapped by chlorophyll and chemical energy trapped into ATP.
7.	A	1	Important to see that X (pyruvate) is a junction for both pathways.
8.	B	1	Decrease in respiration rate can result from a reduction in respiratory substrate as in option B – tricky though.
9.	B	1	Be careful with the **bolds** here.
10.	C	1	Evidence of dominance often comes from looking at phenotypes in the F_1 – the word **all** in option C is a big clue.
11.	C	1	Rough working will be needed here.
12.	B	1	Be aware that flowers take many different forms but the structures are usually in the same positions relative to each other.
13.	C	1	**PS** – **P**hloem carries **S**ugar
14.	A	1	The single un-branched vessel is the lacteal, which leads into the lymph vessels.
15.	D	1	Again, **bio**tic and **bio**logy are related – you are looking for living factors under biotic and non-living ones under abiotic.

Question	Response	Mark	Top Tips
16.	C	1	Make sure you understand how the pyramid shape relates to biomass at the different levels.
17.	A	1	Very tricky – might be useful to mark trends onto the table in the question paper.
18.	A	1	Remember – **I'M** a **N**ew **S**pecies – **I**solation **M**utation **N**atural **S**election.
19.	B	1	A two-step calculation – first find the increase, then divide it by the original value and multiply the answer by 100.
20.	D	1	Tricky – there are **two** variables affecting the result because the disease requires overcrowded conditions to flourish.

Practice Exam B

Section 2

Question			Expected response	Mark	Top Tips
1.	(a)		show smaller vacuole = **1** show cytoplasm/cell membrane pulled from wall = **1**	2	Draw carefully using the shading in cell A as a key for your drawing – sharp pencil needed.
	(b)		turgid	1	Identifying the membrane is vital in seeing what's going on.
	(c)	(i)	osmosis	1	What's moving? If it's water, it's by osmosis!
	(c)	(ii)	does not require (additional) energy	1	Passive is the opposite of active – no additional energy required.
	(d)		tissue similar	1	Cell, tissue, organ, system, organism – levels of organisation again.
2.	(a)		chromatids pulled apart/move toward poles	1	Terms are vital – you will need **chromatid** and **poles**…
	(b)		spindle fibre	1	… and now you need **spindle fibres**.

Question			Expected response	Mark	Top Tips
	(c)		identical diploid unspecialised **All 3 = 2, 2 or 1 = 1**	2	These cells have divided by mitosis so they must be genetically identical and diploid. They can go on to become any of the mature cells of the plant so, at this stage, they must be unspecialised.
3.	(a)		DNA	1	DNA carries the genetic code.
	(b)		1 T/thymine = **1** 2 C/cytosine = **1**	2	Bases are in complementary pairs – you just need to learn them!
	(c)		ribosomes	1	**R**NA goes to **R**ibosomes.
	(d)		the order/sequence of bases	1	The bases are like an alphabet, so their order gives the code its sense.
	(e)		enzyme, hormone, antibody, structural, receptor **any**	1	There are about five different possibilities – learn them!
4.	(a)		scales and labels = **1** plots and connection = **1**	2	Include zeros and highest values on even scales. Include units with labels. Plot with a sharp pencil. Connect plots with straight lines.
	(b)		5:4	1	Make sure you have whole numbers that do not have a common factor.
	(c)		alcohol is toxic to the yeast cells **OR** glucose all used up	1	Standard answer to this question.
	(d)		use a finer scale to measure CO_2 volumes **OR** use a CO_2 probe and data-logger	1	Again, accuracy is related to measurements.
	(e)		repeat but vary the chosen factor and keep all other factors the same	1	Three steps as usual. Repeat, original factor held constant, chosen factor varying.

Question			Expected response	Mark	Top Tips
5.	(a)		electrical impulses	1	Nervous messages are electrical impulses.
	(b)		release of chemical into gap/ synapse		The electrical impulse can be carried through the gap by chemicals.
	(c)		synapse	1	The gaps prevent continuous transmission of nerve impulse – you just have to learn the name.
	(d)		automatic/rapid = **1** protective = **1**	2	The rate of response prevents a harmful stimulus from causing damage.
6.	(a)		1.4 cm	1	Subtract the largest from the smallest.
	(b)		there is a range of lengths involved	1	Remember – continuous variation shows a range of values that merge with each other – the values are not clear-cut.
	(c)		correct matching example, e.g. human tongue-rolling; rose-petal colour	1	Useful to have a few examples up your sleeve – human ones are often easiest to remember.
7.	(a)	(i)	P on left upper vessel on diagram	1	You must learn the pattern – the left atrium position is the reference clue.
	(a)	(ii)	downward arrow	1	Remember the left side is on the right of the diagram! Think about your reflection in a mirror.
	(b)		valves	1	Any type of valve permits one-way flow only.
	(c)		thick wall in arteries, thinner in veins **OR** carry blood away from heart, towards in veins **OR** carry blood under high pressure, lower in veins **OR** veins contain valves, arteries do not	1	There are several differences – you just need to learn them!

Question			Expected response	Mark	Top Tips
	(d)	(i)	haemoglobin present which binds to oxygen = **1**	2	A very specialised protein that can bind but also release oxygen.
	(d)	(ii)	dimples present which give large surface area = **1**		Area is crucial in any absorbing or secreting surface.
8.	(a)		7 until 18 hours	1	Draw a line across the graph from 100 cm³ per hour per plant then read down from the intersects to the times on the scale.
	(b)		1 temperature = **1** 2 light intensity = **1**	2	Looking for environmental factors that vary through a day – these are really the only options. Wind could be involved but it is not a predictable feature of a day.
	(c)		stoma/stomata	1	Remember the pore is the stoma that is formed between the guard cells.
	(d)		carries water to leaves for photosynthesis **OR** cools plant **OR** provides support for cells	1	The standard benefits of transpiration!
9.	(a)		quadrats = **1** drop randomly and count/record numbers of plants inside = **1**	2	Quadrats are the only sampling method for plants mentioned in National 5 assessment. Very simple to use.
	(b)		205	1	Go to the path chart and species 1 – every small box is five plants so 205!
	(c)		species O – decreases in number species P – increases in number **both**	1	Bits of different highlighter colour on the species columns of each graph might help.
	(d)		species Q	1	A bit tricky but species Q stands out as unchanged – in some questions you might have to read the bars carefully.

Question			Expected response	Mark	Top Tips
10.	(a)		**match the name and role** X nitrogen-fixing bacteria = **1** role – convert nitrogen gas into nitrate (in plant) = **1** Y nitrifying bacteria = **1** role – convert ammonia to nitrate in soil = **1** Z denitrifying bacteria = **1** role – convert nitrate to nitrogen gas = **1**	2	There is a choice – probably better to think about each letter in turn and be sure you choose the one you are most confident about.
	(b)		protein, polypeptide, amino acid, nucleic acid	1	Plants take up nitrate, convert it to amino acids, which they use in protein synthesis.
	(c)		fertilisers	1	Fertilisers usually provide NPK – nitrogen, phosphorus and potassium.
11.	(a)		false true true **All 3 = 2, 2/1 = 1**	2	Remember **ROALF** – **R**andom **O**ccurrence **A**nd **L**ow **F**requency. A bit more work needed here though, producing a tricky question.
	(b)		• organisms vary • best adapted varieties have a selective advantage • these varieties survive better • they pass on their genes to their offspring **All 4 = 3, 3 = 2, 2 = 1**	3	Natural selection acts on variation – this is the basis of evolution.
12.	(a)		the further away from the source of pollution, the more lichen cover	1	What do the data show? Is there a trend? Does the trend relate to the statement?
	(b)		8 km	1	Find the high point of the data and read down to the scale.
	(c)		reduce photosynthesis = **1** blockage of light **OR** clogged stomata = **1**	2	Tricky – think about sooty dust and leaves – how could dust affect photosynthesis?

Practice Exam C

Section 1

Question	Response	Mark	Top Tips
1.	D	1	More concentrated in solutes means lower concentration of water so water moves out – that causes the cells to shrink.
2.	A	1	The **p**atchy molecules in the membrane are the **p**roteins.
3.	C	1	Bases are complementary: A always pairs with T, and G always pairs with C.
4.	B	1	Remember, the pH scale measures acidity – the lower the pH number, the more acid. Look for the peaks at the low pH numbers.
5.	B	1	This mainly hinges on knowing that a chromosome is made up of two chromatids, which break apart during mitosis.
6.	C	1	Tricky – the energy in ATP is chemical but it is the energy in light that is required to make it. Water (H_2O) is split into hydrogen and oxygen.
7.	A	1	When the graph slopes, the limiting factor is on the x axis. If the graph line is flat, another factor is limiting – notice the effect of increased temperature at R.
8.	C	1	Remember gluca**gon** is needed when glucose is **gon**e.
9.	D	1	Flowers are different shapes but the internal parts are always laid out in a similar way.
10.	D	1	If a parental characteristic does not show in any of its offspring, then its allele must be recessive.
11.	A	1	You should be able to link the appearance of plant cells with their place in the plant.
12.	C	1	**M**itosis in **M**eristems.
13.	D	1	Link villi with the small intestine then pick out the small intestine in the diagram.
14.	C	1	Remember all respiration starts in the cytoplasm but only aerobic requires further breakdown in the mitochondria.

Question	Response	Mark	Top Tips
15.	B	1	Why not make some flash cards of the terms in this question – the terms come up a lot and can be confusing.
16.	A	1	This is an unusual pyramid and obviously starts with a big plant. The large top often indicates parasites.
17.	A	1	Answer is based on knowing that intraspecific means within the same species. The herring are different stages of the same species.
18.	D	1	Tricky – can be done by eye but better to work out the ratio for each year – this won't take long because the light form is the same each year.
19.	B	1	You need to learn the story here: fertiliser promotes algal growth; aerobic bacteria feed on dead algae and multiply; they deoxygenate water.
20.	B	1	Quite easy if you are careful and read the information given.

Practice Exam C

Section 2

Question			Expected response	Mark	Top Tips
1.	(a)		chloroplasts are present	1	Chloroplasts are the sign of ability to photosynthesise.
	(b)		aerobic respiration **OR** production of ATP	1	Have to recognise the mitochondria and know their function.
	(c)		ribosomes	1	Remember that ribosomes can be attached to a membrane or be free in the cytoplasm.
	(d)		walls composed of different substances **OR** fungal cells don't have chloroplasts	1	You need to know about differences in cell walls and that fungi don't have chloroplasts.

Question			Expected response	Mark	Top Tips
2.	(a)		active transport = **1** low to high concentration **OR** transported by membrane protein = **1**	2	The concentration gradient shown by the molecules in the diagram is the clue!
	(b)	(i)	scales and labels = **1** plots and joining = **1**	2	As usual, remember the basic points.
	(b)	(ii)	osmosis	1	When cells take up water they gain mass.
	(b)	(iii)	1.8 g	1	Get the % increase from the table (90%) then apply it to 2.0 = 1.8 g.
3.	(a)		DNA	1	Genes are made up of DNA (apart from some virus genes, which are RNA).
	(b)		plasmid	1	Plasmids can be removed, altered, then put back into bacterial species.
	(c)		**aseptic techniques** ensures culture not contaminated and desired cell types have no competition from other types **OR** **an appropriate medium** provides nutrients to cells **OR** **control of temperature and pH** provide optimum conditions for enzymes	1	You should try to learn the conditions and techniques for cell culture as a group. Each condition or technique has a biological reason behind it.
	(d)		insulin **OR** growth hormone	1	There are many others but it's probably better to learn these ones.

Question			Expected response	Mark	Top Tips
4.	(a)		8%	1	A two-part calculation: first, take the actual decrease and divide it by the starting length; second, multiply the answer by 100. (4 /50) x 100 = 8%
	(b)		energy in glucose has not been released = **1** ATP is a source of instant energy = **1**	2	The energy in glucose must be released by respiration – this can only happen in live tissue!
	(c)		as a control to show the effects of glucose and ATP	1	The control shows that the factor that was causing the contraction in muscle B was the ATP not the water, which would have been present in the ATP solution.
	(d)		a group of similar cells carrying out the same function	1	Remember the sequence? Organelle – cell – tissue – organ – system – organism.
5.	(a)		A sensory neuron B relay neuron C motor neuron **All 3 = 2, 2 or 1 = 1**	2	The names of the neurons are clues to their functions.
	(b)		heat = **1** (muscular) withdrawal movement = **1**	2	Reflexes are protective so the stimulus is potentially damaging.
	(c)		rapid response provides protection	1	Response has to be rapid because the stimulus will be starting damage immediately. Try **RAP** = **R**apid, **A**utomatic, **P**rotective.
6.	(a)		temperature light intensity watering **1 each, any 2**	2	These are the very basic variables for plant growth – any two will do.
	(b)		43–63 cm	1	The range is the smallest in the sample through to the largest in the sample.

Question			Expected response	Mark	Top Tips
	(c)		gap between tall range and dwarf range caused by genetic differences = **1** range within a variety = **1**	2	In discrete variation there are clear-cut differences – here the cut comes between the tallest dwarf plant and the smallest tall plant!
7.	(a)	(i)	X vena cava = **1** Y coronary artery/vein/vessel = **1**	2	The clue for X is the direction of blood flow. For Y it is the fact that the vessel is attached to the outer surface of the heart.
	(a)	(ii)	true false capillaries false veins **All 3 = 2, 2 or 1 = 1**	2	**A**rteries carry blood **A**way. **V**eins have **V**alves.
	(b)	(i)	0.4 litres	1	Tricky – the 2% has to be applied to the 20 litres inhaled to get the carbon dioxide.
	(b)	(ii)	38 litres	1	For this question, drawing lines on the graph using a ruler will help avoid misreads.
8.	(a)		1 mass of water lost as shown on balance 2 area of leaf to be measured 3 time to be measured **1 each**	3	You need to look at the units of transpiration on the table and think how each part would be measured.
	(b)		repeat the investigation but… alter chosen factor = **1** keep all other factors same = **1**	2	Standard three-step approach needed again – repeat the experiment, keep the original variable constant and vary your chosen factor.
9.	(a)		similar fauna flora climate **1 each**	3	The fauna and flora and climate are similar but <u>not</u> identical
	(b)		38%	1	Just add up the percentages of the different forest-based biomes.
	(c)		role played by an organism	1	A difficult idea so remember the word role as an alternative

Question			Expected response	Mark	Top Tips
10.	(a)		number of traps used method of setting same time of day time left **1 each, any 2**	2	It's really common sense to keep the sampling method the same so that the method does not influence the sample differently for different areas of grassland.
	(b)		not enough traps not randomly set badly set left too long before checking **any = 1**	1	The sources of error are not so much with the traps as with the methods of using them! For example, if the trap lip is above the soil surface or if predators are able to consume the sample!
	(c)		moisture, temperature, pH = **1** moisture meter, thermometer, pH meter/paper = **1**	2	Remember that the instruments are all **meters**.
11.	(a)		isolated populations of finches = **1**		Read the question – what could be stopping interbreeding occurring?
	(b)		different mutations occur in different populations = **1**		It's important to say that mutations are **different**
	(c)		natural selection ensures only best suited organisms survive to breed = **1**	3	It's survival to **breed** which is crucial to evolution
	(b)		neutral	1	Some mutations have little apparent effect on the organism – they are neutral – neither good nor bad.

Question			Expected response	Mark	Top Tips
12.	(a)		formation of nitrates in soil	1	Nitrification is the creation of nitrates in soil – it is essential for soil fertility.
	(b)		1 harvest of crop = **1** 2 leaching to drainage ditch = **1**	2	Anything that removes nitrates or nitrogen-containing substances is a loss to the ecosystem. Crops are harvested so nitrogen is lost in the proteins, etc., which are in the crop plants.
	(c)	(i)	fertiliser application	1	This is the standard way of replacing nitrogen lost in the harvest.
	(c)	(ii)	nodules have nitrogen-fixing bacteria = **1** which convert nitrogen gas into nitrate/ = **1** plough clover into soil	2	In organic farming, fields of clover that have natural nitrogen-fixing bacteria in their roots are grown. The bacteria make nitrates, which are added to the soil when the clover is ploughed.
	(d)		use GM/selectively bred crops **OR** use biological control of pests	1	Intensive farming has led to environmental damage in recent decades, often through the use of chemicals such as fertiliser and pesticides. These methods avoid the use of such chemicals but still produce high yields.